T0046938

"I read a lot of books, and *Holy Sexuality and the Gospel* is on the short-list of most important books I've read in the past decade. There's a desperate need for a biblically astute and theologically grounded yet warm and personal approach to human identity and how it does and doesn't relate to gender and sexuality. This is that book. *Holy Sexuality and the Gospel* is profoundly relevant in an age of toxic confusion. It should be read by every person questioning their sexual identity as well as by every pastor, parent, friend, or sibling."

—RANDY ALCORN, author of *Heaven, Happiness,* and *The Purity
Principle* and director of Eternal Perspective Ministries

"A truly breathtaking book that unpacks the *soul* issues of gender. This book not only gets at the heart of sexuality; it gets at the heart of the gospel. Yuan is an insightful thinker and keen storyteller."

—J. D. GREEAR, PhD, author of *Not God Enough,* sixty-second
president of the Southern Baptist Convention, and pastor of the
Summit Church in Raleigh-Durham, NC

"In a world with many opinions surrounding sexuality, Christopher Yuan has given the church and beyond a resource tethered in something much more concrete—that is, the Word of God. And for that reason, I believe this book can lead many into the truth that will set anybody and everybody free."

—JACKIE HILL-PERRY, poet, speaker, artist, and author of *Gay Girl,
Good God: The Story of Who I Was and Who God Has Always Been*

"Dr. Christopher Yuan has done something deeply and desperately needed: he has told the great story of what the Bible says about sexuality—and about same-sex attractions—in a way that neither compromises the truth nor the love that is at the heart of that story. God's overwhelming love for us is expressed in his passion for us to be holy even as he is holy. So he never calls us to mere celibacy or mere happiness but to a transcendent holiness and joy. That is the fullness and the glory of walking with the God who died for us—and God forbid that we should settle for anything less."

—ERIC METAXAS, *New York Times* best-selling author
of *Bonhoeffer: Prophet, Martyr, Pastor, Spy,* and *Martin Luther: The Man Who Rediscovered God and Changed the World*

"Christopher Yuan is a leader of courage, conviction, and compassion whose life story echoes with amazing grace. This book offers a practical, grounded Christian vision of sexuality in a world culture confused by and obsessed with sex. As the church thinks through how to engage our neighbors on issues such as sexual orientation and gender identity, and on how to disciple our brothers and sisters in Christ who grapple with such temptations, this book will be of immense help."

—RUSSELL MOORE, PhD, president of the Ethics and Religious
Liberty Commission of the Southern Baptist Convention

"What a gift Christopher Yuan is to the body of Christ. His journey into 'a far country' and back home into union with Christ has led him to grapple with hard questions we are all asking (or need to be asking) these days about sexuality, identity, sanctification (both the process and the goal), and what it means to mortify sin and wage war against idols of the heart. In his treatment of these important topics, Christopher is at once humble, compassionate, insightful, and unwaveringly committed to holiness, the authority of Scripture, and the glory of God. Penning this book no doubt required intense exertion and great courage. Thank you, Christopher, for being willing to stay the course—for the sake of us all and, preeminently, for Christ's sake."

—NANCY DEMOSS WOLGEMUTH, author, teacher, and host
of *Revive Our Hearts*

"When it comes to sexuality, singleness, and marriage, we need all the good books we can get. And we certainly need this book from Christopher Yuan. *Holy Sexuality and the Gospel* is part biblical exposition, part theological exploration, and part pastoral exhortation. Christopher has given us a clear-eyed and warm-hearted work that will inspire and encourage the weary as well as instruct and (gently) correct those who have been more shaped by the culture than by the way of Christ."

—KEVIN DEYOUNG, senior pastor of Christ Covenant Church
in Matthews, NC, and assistant professor of systematic theology
at Reformed Theological Seminary in Charlotte, NC

"I'm so very thankful for Christopher Yuan and his faithfulness in the ministry entrusted to him. I'm grateful that he has become a voice of clarity in the midst of so much theological and sexual confusion. I pray that many will heed his clarion call to a holy sexuality."

—TIM CHALLIES, blogger, book reviewer, and author of *Do
More Better*

"If you're looking for a book on what the Bible teaches about sexuality, you've found a good one—one of the best, in fact, that I've read. But this book is so much more. It's an inspiring call to take up our cross and follow Jesus, who's worth everything to those he loves. I'm praying that God will raise up an entire generation like Christopher Yuan, who will lead us in courage and compassion so the world might know that Jesus saves."

—COLLIN HANSEN, editorial director of the Gospel Coalition
and coauthor of *A God-Sized Vision: Revival Stories that
Stretch and Stir*

"*Holy Sexuality and the Gospel* is simply remarkable. This book will reignite your imagination for the gospel and how the gospel shapes our sexuality. Yuan writes with the pen of a theologian, but he also has the heart of someone who knows this issue from personal experience. This book will be required reading for the Transformation Church staff and a resource for our entire church."

—DERWIN L. GRAY, DMIN, lead pastor of Transformation Church in Fort Mill, SC, and author of *Limitless Life: You Are More Than Your Past When God Holds Your Future*

"*Holy Sexuality and the Gospel* is not just a book; it is a treatise on image-bearing, encompassing all of the facets of being human. The writing is compelling yet grounded biblically and theologically. The subject of human sexuality is confusing and divisive in these days. This is a fresh voice and approach including much research, yet it offers examples of living out the truth both personally and for the community of believers—a way forward toward unity."

—JO ANNE LYON, general superintendent emerita and ambassador of the Wesleyan Church

"My friend Christopher Yuan has written a book as biblically sound and culturally self-aware as it is pastorally driven. In *Holy Sexuality and the Gospel,* Christopher understands that cultural debates and scriptural debates are driven by even deeper currents: identity and belief. As Christopher writes, 'The apostle Paul says that in Christ "we live and move and have our being" (Acts 17:28). Thus, my identity is not gay, ex-gay, or even straight. My *true* identity is in Jesus Christ alone.' That's what our society needs to hear. I cannot recommend *Holy Sexuality and the Gospel* highly enough. It is a scandalous book for our age because it calls and draws readers to a bigger horizon than what secularism and theological liberalism offer. The book tackles tough issues ravaging the culture and the local church but does it with a tenor of wisdom and grace."

—ANDREW T. WALKER, PHD, director of policy studies at the Ethics and Religious Liberty Commission and author of *God and the Transgender Debate*

"Does the Bible have anything to say about sexual orientation? Does God call homosexuals to heterosexuality? What do parents do when their child says 'I'm gay'? Christopher Yuan has reduced these complex, controversial questions to one simple answer: 'With same-sex attractions, the problem is sin, and the gospel is the answer.' Christopher is absolutely right: we are called to holiness, to holy sexuality, to reflecting the image of God in every aspect of our lives. This is a clearly written, biblically grounded, theologically sound exposition. It's important reading for singles, for married couples, for pastors, and for all those struggling with same-sex attractions."

—MICHAEL L. BROWN, PhD, host of the *Line of Fire* radio
broadcast and author of *Can You Be Gay and Christian?*

"Christopher Yuan's work tells us that one thing counts most—our identity in Christ and the enablement that comes with it. As he shows, such a focus helps us in all of life, especially in the areas of sexuality, sexual identity, marriage, singleness, and the community that meets needs of intimacy and family. Biblical balance in all of these areas can be a challenge in our culture, especially in knowing how to love and how to converse on these issues. This book does an excellent job of showing the way."

—DARRELL L. BOCK, PhD, executive director for cultural engagement
at the Howard G. Hendricks Center for Christian Leadership
and Cultural Engagement and senior research professor of New
Testament studies at Dallas Theological Seminary, TX

"Dr. Christopher Yuan combines his own gripping story with astute biblically grounded insights into the whole matter of our true identity and its relation to our sexuality. God has a grand design for human flourishing, and this book presents it so engagingly. Dr. Yuan's big idea—clearly written and argued—is holy sexuality as a key to human flourishing. The tone is gracious throughout, and yet the book is uncompromising in its biblical fidelity. I hope that this work is distributed widely and read deeply."

—GRAHAM A. COLE, THD, dean and vice president of education and professor of biblical and systematic theology at Trinity Evangelical Divinity School in Deerfield, IL

Holy Sexuality and the Gospel is a book that must be read by every serious Christian. Yuan brings a wonderful balance of biblical insight and practical application for how Christians can thoughtfully address some of the toughest issues of sex and relationships today. And yet his unflinching commitment to the gospel comes through on every page. I could not recommend the book more highly."

—SEAN MCDOWELL, PHD, associate professor of Christian apologetics at Biola University in La Mirada, CA, speaker, and coauthor of *Evidence That Demands a Verdict*

"This is a book about sexual sanity, and God knows we need it. Our culture has unhinged sexuality from spiritual and biological realities and loaded it with a weight it is not designed to bear. It was never meant to define us. It cannot make our dreams come true. It will not complete us. As a gift of God kept in perspective, sexuality is wonderful. As an idol, it is terrible. More than ever, we need to know what holy sexuality is."

—JON BLOOM, author, board chair, and cofounder of Desiring God

"Christopher Yuan pivots from human sexuality to holy sexuality as he writes with passion and compassion, scholarship and spirituality, personal experience and practical expertise."

—LEITH ANDERSON, DMIN, president of the National Association of Evangelicals

FOREWORD by ROSARIA BUTTERFIELD

HOLY SEXUALITY AND THE GOSPEL

Sex, Desire, and Relationships Shaped by God's Grand Story

CHRISTOPHER YUAN

MULTNOMAH

Holy Sexuality and the Gospel

All Scripture quotations are taken from the Holy Bible, English Standard Version, ESV® Text Edition® (2016), copyright © 2001 by Crossway Bibles, a publishing ministry of Good News Publishers. All rights reserved.

Details in some anecdotes and stories have been changed to protect the identities of the persons involved.

Trade Paperback ISBN 978-0-7352-9091-4
eBook ISBN 978-0-7352-9092-1

Cover design by Kelly L. Howard

Published in the United States by Multnomah, an imprint of the Crown Publishing Group, a division of Penguin Random House LLC, New York.

MULTNOMAH® and its mountain colophon are registered trademarks of Penguin Random House LLC.

Library of Congress Cataloging-in-Publication Data
Names: Yuan, Christopher, author.
Title: Holy sexuality and the Gospel : sex, desire, and relationships shaped by God's grand story / Christopher Yuan.
Description: First Edition. | Colorado Springs : Multnomah, 2018. | Includes bibliographical references.
Identifiers: LCCN 2018015755| ISBN 9780735290914 (pbk.) | ISBN 9780735290921 (electronic)
Subjects: LCSH: Sex—Religious aspects—Christianity.
Classification: LCC BT708 .Y83 2018 | DDC 261.8/357—dc23
LC record available at https://lccn.loc.gov/2018015755

Printed in the United States of America
2023

20 19 18 17 16 15 14 13

SPECIAL SALES
Most Multnomah books are available at special quantity discounts when purchased in bulk by corporations, organizations, and special-interest groups. Custom imprinting or excerpting can also be done to fit special needs. For information, please email specialmarketscms@penguin randomhouse.com or call 1-800-6037051.

For Mom.

Thank you for being my childhood heroine,
for teaching me to be tenacious and never to
settle for mediocrity. Thank you in my adult
years for being a trailblazer, setting true north
on the perfect image of God, who is Christ.
This book on holiness is dedicated to you.

Contents

Foreword

In 2011 Christopher Yuan coauthored with his mother, Angela Yuan, a striking, transparent memoir entitled *Out of a Far Country: A Gay Son's Journey to God, a Broken Mother's Search for Hope.* No memoir has impacted my life more personally.

When this book was published, Christian culture routinely (and robotically) talked about being "delivered out of homosexuality." In stark contrast, *Out of a Far Country* revealed that Christopher, like all true followers of Jesus Christ, was converted—not out of homosexuality but out of unbelief. Only because the gospel of Jesus Christ changed Christopher from the inside out, making him a new man in Christ, was he able to do what all converts do: kill our idols, including the idol of a sexual sin that has called our names from our earliest memories. That powerful memoir revealed that living like a Christ follower is not a moralistic hack job. It is dying to self so that you can live for Christ. In the very end of this faithful book, Christopher introduced the concept of "holy sexuality," a concept that changed the paradigm of what it means to live out God's best for us.

But a memoir is provincial by definition and often leaves the reader with more questions than it offers answers. What is holy sexuality? Isn't it better to be married than single (even though the Bible says just the opposite)? Isn't it better to be heterosexual than homosexual (even though the Bible refuses to define personhood in Freudian terms)? Isn't a Christian delivered out of homosexuality (even though the Bible makes clear that Christians will struggle against all manner of sin in this lifetime and that struggling with Christ's power to mortify sin and repent of it gives glory to God)? In *Holy Sexuality and the Gospel,* Dr. Yuan, in his characteristic warm, engaging, theologically sound, and utterly practical way, offers guidance on these and many other matters.

Since the fall of Adam, the human heart has set itself in defiance against God's authority. This defiance has taken different forms throughout the ages. In the not-so-distant past, we blamed the devil for our sinful sexual passions ("The devil made me do it"). With the onset of the theological negligence of neo-orthodoxy, we have created a generation of Christians who blame the Holy Spirit for their sinful desires ("God made me this way, and it's a proof of good fruit when I act in accordance with my heart's desires"). Thus, from the epoch of late modernity onward, the gospel is on a collision course with the idol of sexual freedom.

This is an issue not only for those who struggle with same-sex attractions or for those who love someone who identifies as LGBTQ. This is an issue for all of us. We all must wage holy war against the idols of our hearts. The idol of our historical epoch is this: your sexual desires define you, determine you, and should always delight you.

Dr. Yuan shows us how deeply dangerous this position is and where it will lead us. He shows how this unbiblical theology weakens our ability to love the Lord, trust his moral law, live in the vitality of the Holy Spirit, and apply the habits of grace needed in times of trial (including the trial of shaking the gates of heaven with prayer for loved ones whose desires of the flesh are clobbering them fast and furiously).

In this light, *Holy Sexuality and the Gospel* helps the reader navigate some of the new vocabulary of the day, introduced after the 2015 Supreme Court case (*Obergefell v. Hodges*) legalized same-sex marriage in all fifty states. He tackles head-on the hardest and most pressing questions: What is wrong with using therapy to "change" sexual orientation? Does sexual orientation reveal who I really am at my deepest core? If I still struggle against same-sex sexual desires, am I a gay Christian? How do I love my adult children well who identify as gay and are giving me ultimatums about an upcoming wedding?

Dr. Yuan shows us how to think biblically and act with moral clarity. Christians must deal daily with the original sin that corrupts us, the actual sin that distracts and enlists us, and the indwelling sin that manipulates us. *Holy Sexuality and the Gospel* shows how to use the tools that God has given us to give God glory in our confession and repentance. Christians must learn how to hate our sin without hating ourselves. *Holy Sexuality and the Gospel* shows us how our union with Christ delivers Christ's risen power as we deny our deep desires for the sake of something better.

This book is a tour de force of theological integrity and hope for sexual strugglers and for those who stand beside them. This book never sacrifices sound biblical theology for personal experience, but it also never dismisses the power and importance of personal experience. Every page drips with love for God, love for our neighbors, and love for the church. The love that you find here is vital, biblical love. It's the kind of love the world knows not. I refer here to the Love that came with sacrificial blood, unimaginable pain, heartless betrayal, and eternal joy for those who stand in the risen Christ alone.

Read this book. It will bring biblical clarity, practical theology, pastoral guidance, and personal testimony to bear on this truth of gospel life: that dying to self and living for Christ is hero's work, and with God's help, it is the only way forward for ourselves, our lost loved ones, and our hurting world.

The Bible is the most important book the world has for all generations. The Bible is our guide to faith and life. Nothing can compete with it or improve it. But in Dr. Christopher Yuan's *Holy Sexuality and the Gospel,* you are holding in your hands the most important humanly composed book about biblical sexuality and godly living for our times.

—Rosaria Butterfield

1

SHAPED BY GOD'S GRAND STORY

Framing the Conversation with Theology

"I am gay" is a simple statement with a complex and multifaceted meaning. We all know someone who's gay. You most likely picked up this book because you have a gay child, sibling, coworker, or dear friend.

As a follower of Christ, you recognize that John 3:16—"*For God so loved the world*"—includes this individual. Your love for him or her is not in question. Rather, the question is, What does this love look like?

Many books provide advice for showing compassion to those experiencing same-sex attractions. They offer different and sometimes conflicting approaches on how to do this. Do we help gays and lesbians embrace their sexuality and encourage a modern church "reformation" that affirms same-sex marriage? Do we help heal a torn church by advocating for unity between "affirming" and "nonaffirming" sides?

Do we help gay Christians cultivate deeply spiritual friendships while they accept a stark reality of lifelong celibacy? Do we help those with unwanted same-sex attractions fulfill their heterosexual potential and marry someone of the opposite sex? Or could the gospel be calling us *all* to something costlier but more magnificent than we've ever envisioned?

The diverse approaches in these books all begin with a common intent: love. The difference is not just methodology, but it stems from varying definitions of *love*. In fact, many well-intentioned pastors who preach fire-and-brimstone sermons against the gay community *believe* they're doing it out of love—albeit a deeply misguided love and a lop-sided view of the gospel.

With so many methods, which is the right one? Discerning the correct way to love is not a theoretical exercise. For me, it's deeply personal.

This Is My Song

In 1993 I announced to my parents that I was gay. This led to massive disruption in our family, to put it lightly. Ultimately, this moment became a catalyst that led each of us, one by one, to the Lord.

At the time, my unbelieving mom rejected me. But contrary to the stereotype, after she became a Christian, she knew she could do nothing other than love her gay son as God loved her.

However, with no more secrets, I felt unimpeded to fully embrace "who I was." This new freedom quickly propelled me down a path of self-destruction that included promiscuity and illicit drug use. Certainly, not all gay men go down this road, but it was my reality. Ultimately, I was expelled from dental school in Louisville, moved to Atlanta, and became a supplier to drug dealers in more than a dozen states.

During this time God graciously worked in the lives of my father and mother and brought them both to a saving trust in Christ. My parents didn't realize the extent of my rebellion, but in the light of their new-found faith, they knew my biggest sin wasn't same-sex sexual behavior; my biggest sin was unbelief. What I needed more than anything else, through God's gift of grace, was faith to believe and follow Jesus.

My mother began to pray a bold prayer: "Lord, do whatever it takes to bring this prodigal son to you." She didn't pray primarily for me to come home to Chicago or to stop my rebellious behavior. Her main request was that God would draw me to himself and that I would fall into his loving arms as his son, adopted and purchased by the blood of the Lamb.

The answer to her prayers came in an unexpected way: I was arrested for drug dealing. In jail, I experienced the darkest moments of my life when I received news that I was HIV positive. That night, as I lay in a prison cell bed, I noticed something scribbled on the metal bunk above me: "If you're bored, read Jeremiah 29:11." So I did and was intrigued by the promise I read there: "'I know the plans I have for you,' declares the Lord, 'plans for welfare and not for evil, to give you a future and a hope.'"

I read the Bible more and more. As I did, I realized I'd placed my identity in the wrong thing. The world tells those of us with same-sex attractions that our sexuality is the core of who we are. But God's Word paints quite a different picture. Genesis 1:27 informs us that we are all created in the image of God. The apostle Paul says that in Christ "we live and move and have our being" (Acts 17:28). Thus, my identity is not gay, ex-gay, or even straight. My *true* identity is in Jesus Christ alone.

Ultimately, upon my release from jail, I committed to studying and submitting to biblical and theological truth. I enrolled in Bible college and later, seminary. Over time, God has given back the years the locusts had taken away (Joel 2:25). My parents and I now travel around the world as a two-generational ministry, communicating God's grace and God's truth on biblical sexuality.

Meaning to Method

Through my journey from agnostic gay man to evangelical Bible professor, I've come to realize that the differences in how people respond to gay and same-sex-attracted individuals are rooted in *meaning*. From ancient times, humanity has been pursuing meaning. And out of meaning flow actions.

Our divergent approaches on how to love the gay community—stemming from competing interpretations of meaning—can be overwhelming and confusing. Clarity comes not by trying to decide which approach is more compassionate but by observing which approach is grounded in the correct version of truth—God's truth. With good intentions, we may rush into doing "what's right," but if we don't begin with *right thinking,* there's a good chance we could be doing what's wrong.

Both compassion and wisdom are virtues. But compassion without wisdom can be careless, even reckless. Wisdom without compassion is useless, even pharisaical. True compassion flows from wisdom, and true wisdom results in compassion—there should be no dichotomy. The real Christian life is built on godly wisdom.

We're often encouraged in our society to embrace relevance and pragmatism at the expense of truth. But correct practice flows from correct truth. We must resist the natural impulse to disjoin practice from truth or truth from practice.

Certainly, there's great importance in exploring the ethics of same-sex relationships, and many scholars have written about the key Old and New Testament passages prohibiting same-sex sexual practice. This work is vital, and several books have done it well.[1]

However, we limit ourselves if we think that "right knowing" simply means studying a handful of biblical texts relevant to the topic at hand. This would be missing the forest for the trees. A robust theology cannot be built on what we're *not* allowed to do, for the Christian life is much more than the avoidance of sinful behavior. If scriptural prohibitions are the only lens through which we see things, then we may well miss the gospel.

My goal for this book is to provide both theological reflection on sexuality and practical action points for those of us trying to share Christ with our gay loved ones through the lens of God's grand story—creation, fall, redemption, and consummation. You may be thinking, *I'm no theologian!* but the Greek word *theologia* literally means "knowledge of God." Do you have any knowledge of God? If so, you're a theologian!

Kevin Zuber, a professor of mine in Bible college, deeply impacted me when he challenged the class to think about theology as a verb. Christians are supposed to *do* theology. Theology *done* well engages heart, mind, and hands. Anemic theology breeds apathy, but good theology compels action.

Even still, you may be thinking, *What I need right now is not theology but practical advice on how to better minister to my gay loved ones and friends.* Yet how can we know what God wants for our gay friends without ample knowledge of God? Thoughts precede action.

Good theology, right action. Bad theology, wrong action.

Breaking Bad Paradigms

In 2011 I coauthored a book with my mother, Angela, entitled *Out of a Far Country: A Gay Son's Journey to God, a Broken Mother's Search for Hope.*[2] Toward the end of our memoir, I briefly introduced the concept of *holy sexuality.*

The impetus for this new phrase stemmed from my frustration with the heterosexual-bisexual-homosexual paradigm, particularly its incongruence with biblical and theological truth. I knew that at some point I needed to flesh out this important biblical definition of *holy sexuality.*

Over the years, I came to understand that the goal of holy sexuality is not just for those who experience attractions toward people of the same sex; holy sexuality is for everyone. This understanding of sexuality is tethered to God's grand story—creation, fall, redemption, and consummation. This full-orbed, coherent theological framework helps us better and more fully comprehend human sexuality in light of God's revealed truth.

Will you join me on a journey as we investigate a theology of sexuality? As we go, be prepared to think biblically, theologically, and critically; to challenge some of our old human-made paradigms not grounded in Scripture; and, in some situations, to change and realign to God's truth.

As always, don't resist the Holy Spirit as he convicts us of wrong thinking and even as he grants us the gracious gift of repentance. Get ready for us to deepen our knowledge of God and his grand story, which will then rightly shape our understanding of human sexuality.

Are you ready?

A CASE OF MISTAKEN IDENTITY

Is Sexuality Who We Really Are?

"This is who I am." The words were spoken by Andy, one of my class-mates from seminary. He and I and another friend occasionally debated Bible passages after class—just for fun. Andy was a bright young man, raised on the mission field, and married to a godly young lady. So I was surprised when I heard that Andy had come out of the closet and was no longer living with his wife. It had been his secret, and many close to him felt blindsided by the news.

As we got together to discuss the Bible that week, our dialogue inevi-tably turned to texts related to homosexuality. It became apparent as we talked that a shift in Andy's hermeneutics had occurred. His flippant dismissal of biblical authors as ignorant or simply uninformed gave evi-dence that he had changed his views regarding biblical authority and inerrancy.

We'd been challenging each other for about an hour when Andy suddenly thrust our conversation in a different direction entirely, from theoretical to intensely personal: "Why would God make me this way and then not allow me to be who I am? For years, I prayed for God to take this away and change me. Nothing happened, and nothing will. I've been denying this for far too long. I never chose this. I just have to be honest and authentic and accept the truth that I'm gay. This is who I am."

At that point, I knew from personal experience that the issue went beyond Andy's incorrect interpretations of Bible passages relating to same-sex relationships. It was more profound than simply bad exegesis or a low view of Scripture. Andy's words revealed a deeper philosophical and theological misunderstanding, a faulty presupposition that pointed to his essence, to the core of his being: *This is who I am.*

Being gay is no longer what I'm attracted to, what I desire, or what I do—it's *who I am.* Matthew Vines, a gay activist, writes that sexual attraction "is simply part of who you are" and "as humans, our sexuality is a core part of who we are."[1] In the conversation around sexuality, this subtle shift from *what* to *who* has created a radically distorted view of personhood.[2]

There is no other sin issue so closely linked to identity. For example, being a gossiper is not who he is but what he does. Or being an adulteress is not who she is but what she does. Being a hater is not who he is but what he does. Should the capacity for same-sex attractions really describe who I am at my most basic level? Or should it describe *how* I am? Might this be a categorical fallacy that ultimately distorts how we think and live? The terms *heterosexual* and *homosexual* turn desire into personhood, experience into ontology.

My friend Andy's statement, which is similar to that of many gays and lesbians, brings to the forefront an age-old question: *Who am I?* From Plato to Descartes, from Kant to Foucault, philosophers throughout history have attempted to shed light on this profound mystery.

Philosophers aren't the only ones who've asked that question. We've all asked it. During puberty, teenagers especially struggle with their identity, and middle-aged adults commonly question their existence and meaning. For many, the search for identity can last a lifetime.

For some, self-identity is shaped by family, friends, and culture. Others find their identity in work, in sports or hobbies, or in the latest trending activism. Some find their sole identity in being a parent. Still others, as we know, find their identity in their sexuality.

Do these substitutes for identity truly describe who we are or only what we do or experience? And specifically, does sexuality describe *who* we are or does it really explain *how* we are? Our answers to these questions affect many facets of our lives. It impacts the way we think, the choices we make, and the relationships we build.

All our thoughts and actions are influenced at some level by how we answer the question *Who am I?* This suggests a closer relationship between *essence* and *ethics* than many realize. The two inform each other. Who we are (essence) determines how we live (ethics), and how we live determines who we are.[3]

If we have a flawed view of who we are, we'll have a flawed personal ethic, and if we have a flawed personal ethic, we'll have a flawed view of who we are. Personhood affects practice, and practice affects personhood.

When I came out in my early twenties, I believed the only way to live authentically as a gay man was to fully embrace that identity. Being gay was who I was. As a matter of fact, my whole world was gay. Almost everyone I knew was gay.

All my friends were gay. My neighbors were gay. My apartment manager was gay. My barber was gay. My house cleaner was gay. My bookkeeper was gay. My car salesman was gay. I worked out at a gay gym and bought groceries at the gay Kroger.

Sexuality was the core of who I was, and everything and everyone around me affirmed that. And if *I am gay* truly means that's *who I am,* it would be utterly cruel for someone to condemn me for simply being myself.

Yet we know that we are created in God's image (Genesis 1:27).

Thus, rejecting our inherent essence and replacing it simply with what we feel or do is in reality an attempted coup d'état against our Creator. We don't need to find our identity; our identity is given by God.[4]

But why isn't this apparent to everyone? What causes our gay loved ones to be so easily misled? Why does my gay Christian friend identify more with being gay than being Christian? Where and when did this incorrect perspective originate? How did *what I do* and *what I feel* become *who I am*? Or, to put it another way, how did "This is *how* I am" become "This is *who* I am"?

Potential and Peril

Prior to the mid-1800s, sexuality was understood strictly as behavior, not identity. No word existed to describe an individual with same-sex attractions. Sigmund Freud and his contemporaries were the first to introduce terms to categorize people according to their sexual attractions—*heterosexual* and *homosexual*.

In 1870 German psychiatrist Carl Westphal was the earliest to utilize *homosexuality* as a way to characterize a person's nature, not just his sexual practice.[5] German psychiatrist Richard von Krafft-Ebing wrote one of the first works on sexual pathology and homosexuality, published in 1886.[6] The popularity of Krafft-Ebing's book made the words he used in it to describe sexual orientation—*heterosexual* and *homosexual*—more mainstream.

Sigmund Freud (1856–1939) had an immense impact on the discussion of homosexuality and sexual orientation. Freud's most important articles on homosexuality were written between 1905 and 1922. Unlike his peers, he viewed homosexuality not as a sickness but as an inversion. Homosexual was just another variety of humanity. Thus, heterosexual and homosexual became new, secular categories for personhood.

This concept of identity, based on feelings and behavior, blossomed in the fertile soil of burgeoning secular philosophies. Europe in the 1800s had experienced a movement within art, literature, music, and academic thought known as Romanticism. Reacting to the rationalism[7] of the Enlightenment as well as the herd mentality of the Industrial Revolution, Romanticism extolled emotions and individualism.

It revered senses over intellect, emotions over reason. A key component of Romanticism was the assumption that humans are inherently good, and if humans are inherently good, then human emotions (feelings, affections, desires, etc.) are also inherently good.

Along with Romanticism, the philosophy of *existentialism* was a rising force in Europe, placing priority on freedom and a strong emphasis on living, acting, and feeling. Existentialism's highest virtue was authenticity.

Søren Kierkegaard (1813–55), generally regarded as the first existentialist thinker, believed that truth could be discovered only subjectively via one's actions and that, from those actions, each individual had the difficult but essential duty of finding meaning and creating value and personal identity.

Taken to its end, existentialism inevitably led to *nihilism*—the idea that life has no inherent meaning or value. Friedrich Nietzsche (1844–1900), best known for his audacious claim that "God is dead," railed against Christianity. He believed the individual must break free from the moral constraints of society (particularly religion) to create oneself anew.

And why not? Without any intrinsic value or objective meaning in life, the individual must reevaluate existence and courageously live according to his or her own desires. If there's no God, there's no essence; identity must be created by each person. And if there's no essence—only existence—then ethics has no mooring and must also be created.

The strong influence of these philosophies and movements on Western culture produced a vacuum. In the absence of any objective foundation for true identity, experience essentially became God. Experience reigned supreme, and everything else had to bow before it. *Sola experientia* ("experience alone") won out over *sola Scriptura* ("Scripture alone"). In such a climate, the idea that sexuality represents our core identity quickly took root.

I know firsthand how easy it is to allow emotions and desires to become the bedrock of who I am, just as my friend Andy had thoroughly convinced himself after years of inner struggle that no other explanation existed. His experience had subsumed personhood; *what I feel* had become *who I am.*

Know Thyself

In the face of today's widespread belief that experience supersedes essence, the correct way for Christians to comprehend identity—particularly as it relates to sexuality—is to better grasp who we are in light of God's truth. True identity is not *what* I do (for example, I am a writer). Nor is it *how* I am (for example, I am happy). True identity is *who* I am. In other words, identity in Christ means union with Christ.

We cannot properly understand human sexuality unless we begin with *theological anthropology.* Anthropology, in general terms, is the study of humanity. Essentially, it's the human search to answer the important question, Who am I?

Most anthropologists begin with the incorrect premise that there is no God. But an incorrect premise obscures the truth, resulting in conclusions that are intrinsically limited at best or completely mistaken and deceiving at worst. A true, faithful, and accurate anthropology begins with God.

The reformer John Calvin articulated this profound truth: "Man never achieves a clear knowledge of himself unless he has first looked upon God's face."[8] When secular researchers reject the supernatural, it's no surprise that they also disregard the possibility of *purpose* behind the origin of human beings. Christians know there *is* a God who lovingly and intentionally created us for a purpose.

We begin with a completely theocentric, or God-centered, view of humankind—that we're all created in the image of God (Genesis 1) but also distorted by sin because of the Fall (Genesis 3). Only then are we able to understand our desires, submit to Christ, and live according to God's will.

Who am I? Who are you? Who are they? Who are we? The answer begins with the image of God and the doctrine of sin.

THE IMAGE OF GOD

Where Identity Begins

A persistent beep went off every few moments next to his head. It was muffled at first but gradually became more annoying. *What's that sound?* His body was sluggish; he tried moving his arms to his face but couldn't. A mental fog made it extremely difficult to bring his fragmented thoughts into coherence.

Where am I? He opened his eyes and winced at the light. As he tried to move his arms again, he noticed that he was strapped to the bed. Panic filled his mind, and his heart raced. The beeping next to his head grew louder and faster.

A nurse ran into the room and tried to calm him down. He tried to speak but couldn't—it was as if he no longer knew how to put words together. All that came out were moans. Thrashing about, he tried to break free. The nurse shouted; then others quickly appeared beside the bed, pressing him down.

What are you doing to me? Who are you? Why am I here?

Unfortunately, this confusion from severe memory loss and impaired motor skills continued for weeks. Using words and making decisions were difficult for him. The slow and arduous road to mental and physical recovery lasted several months.

This patient was David Wheeler, my good friend and classmate at

Moody Bible Institute. After graduating, he became a missionary in the Middle East with Operation Mobilization for two years. While staying with his parents on furlough, he suffered a massive heart attack stemming from a congenital heart condition.

His parents were away that morning, but David was able to call an ambulance before falling unconscious. With prolonged oxygen deprivation to his brain, he experienced severe short- and long-term memory loss. He didn't know his own name, his age, his home address, his phone number, his parents' names, or even the year. This was the reality: David had no idea who he was.

To make matters worse, somehow David's wallet and identification were misplaced—possibly even stolen—at the public hospital where he was taken. Having been back from the Middle East for only a few days, he still had his long hair and beard, looking a bit like a displaced vagabond.

So for many days, because of the posttraumatic amnesia and bizarre combination of factors, David had no name or legal identity and was presumed to be a deadbeat homeless man—and was treated as such. His hospital patient records simply read "John Doe."

David's parents had no clue about their son's heart attack or his stay in the public hospital. They assumed he'd gone to visit friends. When he hadn't returned home or called, they began to worry. It took several days for his parents to find out what had happened. David Wheeler didn't know who he was. And without a true identity, he was lost and essentially nonexistent.

Sadly, many of us go through life not knowing our true identity, all the while embracing an incorrect one. As with David, we're lost without our true identity. What's worse is that many of us don't even know it. We may know our name, our address, our family's and friends' names—but do we really know who we are in God's eyes? If we don't, how can we understand anything related to the human condition?

It's no wonder confusion abounds when it comes to human sexuality—we don't even know who we are. But the truth is, we can't properly understand human sexuality unless we begin with theological anthropology.

If *human* sexuality is our subject, it's critical to understand what the Bible says about *humanity*. And to understand humanity, the starting point is God—whose thoughts are higher than our thoughts (Isaiah 55:9) and who therefore provides an impartial point of view unlimited by the finitude of human knowledge.

Only God comprehensively and exhaustively understands us because he created us and knows all things. As a matter of fact, an important premise of theological anthropology is recognizing that "Know thyself" isn't possible apart from God. Thus, the Christian approach to anthropology and to human sexuality emerges from the doctrine of God found in his Word.

For our discussion on sexuality, two important aspects of theological anthropology are the image of God (*imago Dei*) and the doctrine of sin. These two doctrines may seem distinct—one good, one bad—but they're intimately linked. If they're separated, false teachings are inevitable.

The image of God without the Fall leads to universalism (the belief that all humanity is eventually granted eternal life with God), while the doctrine of sin without the *imago Dei* leads to legalistic moralism. These theological doctrines derive from the beginning, and that's where we'll start.

Imagining the Beginning

"Then God said, 'Let us make man in our image, after our likeness. . . .' So God created man in his own image, in the image of God he created him; male and female he created them" (Genesis 1:26–27).

The doctrine of the image of God is essential to understanding what human sexuality truly is and who we are as human beings. In the opening chapter of Genesis, God created Adam and Eve as the crown of all creation in his own image. The *imago Dei* concept is then repeated in Genesis 5:1 and 9:6: "When God created man, he made him in the likeness of God" and "Whoever sheds the blood of man, by man shall his blood be shed, for God made man in his own image."

Scholars have discussed and debated for centuries the various aspects of the image of God.[1] Some mistakenly say that we *have* the image of God or that the image of God is *in* us. Yet the Bible doesn't express it in this way. As Bible scholar and translator Moisés Silva explains, "Man *as a whole,* male and female, is described as being made in God's image."[2]

If we misidentify the image of God as something *in* us, we'll mistake it for some human aspect or characteristic (such as soul, spirit, relational capacity, etc.). Silva further articulates this comprehensive nature: "*Every* aspect of human beings is a reflection of the divine image."[3] The focus of the *imago Dei* doctrine is on the human being in totality.

Within that totality, God has given human beings divine characteristics. Although tainted by sin, all our human qualities—not just some—are reflections of God's attributes. Old Testament scholar Bruce Waltke provides rationale for this by stating that we're "made like God so that God can communicate himself to people."[4]

Therefore, when we make anything else the core of our being—especially our sexuality—it's not only a distortion of the *imago Dei* but also an affront to our Creator. Mis-imaging God should never be treated as trivial, benign, or inconsequential.

Outside the book of Genesis, the Hebrew word *image* has a negative connotation since it refers to some form of a human-made idol. Just as graven images are reflections of false gods, *we* are representations of the one true God and intentionally created to be like him. Wayne Grudem explains, "The fact that man is in the image of God means that man is like God and represents God."[5]

The image of God is intrinsic to being human. Let's explore four salient realities of the *imago Dei,* each of which has important implications regarding human sexuality.

The Image of God Is Very Good

Before creating male and female, God created the heavens and the earth, filling the earth with vegetation and living creatures. In the creation narrative, as God was bringing things into existence, we read this affirmation six times: "God saw that it was good."[6] Everything he created in the entire material world was good and worthy of praise.

Yet God's highest acclaim was withheld for the apex of creation, when he created humankind in his own image and blessed them, male and female. The entire creation narrative culminates with "Behold, it was very good" (Genesis 1:31). *Very* good.

This word for "good" is less about aesthetics and more about purpose;[7] humanity, like all of creation, was created *for* good. It's safe to say that any goodness in us can be attributed only to God.

In their state of innocence, Adam and Eve lived in perfect, voluntary obedience to God—but only for a time. Genesis 3 gives the sad account of their free and voluntary disobedience to God, which cast the human race into the sinful state.

Although humankind fell into sin, the image of God was only distorted, not lost. The *imago Dei* was effaced but not eradicated. And the good news is the promise of glorification in which God's faithful ones will no longer sin or even struggle with sin (Revelation 21:27). For now, our fallenness is only temporary; it isn't an integral aspect of who we are.

The truth of the matter is that sin and its consequences are subsidiary rather than essential to being human.[8] Sin is universal and pervasive, but it isn't *who* we are. Every sinful person is still a person created in God's image. Regardless of anyone's age, sex, or race; regardless of whether one is in submission to God or not; and regardless of whether a person experiences same-sex attraction or identifies as gay or lesbian—everyone is created in the *imago Dei*. It's inherent to who we are and is never erased.

When we say that every person should be treated with dignity and respect, it's not because of our commitment to human rights but because we're all created in the image of God. Every person is endowed with inestimable value and should be treated with dignity and respect. The *imago Dei* is the only true foundation of human rights.

This is an indictment of Christians who mock or demonize people identifying as gay, lesbian, bisexual, or transgender. Such hurtful actions and attitudes fail to honor the dignity and value of others created in the image of God. It also forsakes the believer's calling to reflect the image of Christ and proclaim the good news to those who have yet to believe.

The Image of God Is Unique

God created all things, but no other being was created in his image—not even angels. Plants and animals were all created "according to their kinds,"[9] but with human beings, God did something quite different. From the dust of the ground (*adamah* in Hebrew), he formed man (*adam*) and breathed into him so that "man became a living creature" (Genesis 2:7). It's astonishing to consider: the breath that brought man to life parallels the Scripture "breathed out by God" who gives us eternal life (2 Timothy 3:16).

No other creature has this same privilege. Animals were never created in God's image, and therefore, human beings can never be considered as simply a higher-developed form of animal life. We're distinct from all other life, and the secular world's efforts to make humanity equivalent to the animal kingdom are misguided and misleading.

Likewise, the attempt to justify human same-sex relationships by referring to the "natural" occurrence of homosexuality among animals reflects a low anthropology in which humans are no different from beasts. It's quite simple: don't take your moral cues from animals. After all, some animals cannibalize one another and even eat their own young!

Being made in the image of God differentiates us from everything else in God's created world. What an amazing and humbling reality!

The Image of God Is Male and Female

Genesis 1:27 conveys an undeniable connection between the *imago Dei* and the ontological categories of male and female. Analyzing this verse through the lens of rhetorical analysis reveals an indelible link between the image of God and sexual differentiation.

In Genesis 1:27 we find these three parallel lines of poetry:

> So God created man in his own image,
>> in the image of God he created him;
>> male and female he created them.

The first line lays the foundation on which the next two lines build— the fact that "God created man in his own image." The second line basically repeats the first but in different order: the prepositional phrase ("in the image of God") is at the beginning, and the subject-verb-object ("he created him") is at the end.

The third line also ends with the subject-verb-object: "he created them." But now the singular pronoun "him" in line two has been replaced by the plural "them." The singular and plural pronouns in these two lines echo the preceding verse in which God himself is expressed as both singular and plural: "Then God said, 'Let us make . . . ' "[10] The inherent relationality and fellowship within the Godhead are reflected in the inherent relationality and fellowship within humankind.[11]

But the biggest surprise in verse 27 is at the start of that third line: the noun pair "male and female" takes the place of the second line's prepositional phrase "in the image of God." The second and third lines are poetically structured in parallel, communicating a direct correlation between the image of God and male and female.

The Hebrew language sometimes utilizes threefold repetition as one of its most explicit superlatives—for example, "Holy, holy, holy" from Isaiah 6:3. The three parallel lines of Genesis 1:27 in immediate succession cause the listener to pause and take notice of this profound truth on the image of God and sexual differentiation. Just as the image of God is essential to who we are, male or female is essential to who we are.

This is not to say that God *is* male or female or both. In actuality, the creation narrative in Genesis 1 conveys the exact opposite message—it was a polemic against false gods. According to ancient Near Eastern pagan mythology, all came into being through the sexual union of a male god and a female god.

But Scripture tells us that along with making the heavens and the earth, God created sexual differentiation, and he thus stands above the polarity of sex. God is neither male nor female. Richard Davidson explains in his book *Flame of Yahweh: Sexuality in the Old Testament,* "The sexual distinctions are presented as a creation by God, not part of the divine realm."[12] Therefore, it's a bit inane to suggest that God is transgender or gender-fluid, as purported by Rabbi Mark Sameth.[13] Simply put, God transcends male and female.

Differentiation is a fundamental recurring element in creation. God separated light and darkness, day and night, evening and morning, the waters and the heavens, land and sea. He created plants and trees "each according to its kind" and also all fish and birds and land animals "according to their kinds."[14] Likewise, God differentiated humanity and uniquely created them in his own image "male and female."

The *imago Dei* and being male or female are essential to being human. As hard as anyone may try to alter that fact in his or her own body, the most that can be done is to artificially remove or augment body parts or use pharmaceuticals to unnaturally suppress the biological reality of one's essence as male or female. When denying this physical and genetic reality, we let experience supersede essence—*what I feel is who I am*. In other words, psychology usurps biology.

When anyone embraces this ideology, truth is no longer absolute. Truth becomes what I think and what I feel. Transgenderism is not only a battle of ontology (the study of being) but also a battle of epistemology (the study of knowledge). No matter what the world teaches, sexual differentiation is not a social construct. Being male or female is an intrinsic aspect of who we are.

The Image of God Is Christological

In the arc of God's grand story, we've seen how the image of God in humanity was perverted (though not lost) when Adam and Eve fell into disobedience. Sin, death, judgment, and condemnation came through the first Adam, but righteousness, life, atonement, and justification came through the last Adam, who is Jesus Christ (Romans 5:12–21; 1 Corinthians 15:45–49).

In and through Christ we see the image of God being restored to its original purity and glory. In Colossians 1:15, Paul writes that Jesus "is the image of the invisible God, the firstborn of all creation." The writer of

Hebrews states that Jesus "is the radiance of the glory of God and the exact imprint of his nature" (Hebrews 1:3). Jesus is God's perfect image.

However, from Romans 1:21 we see that sin has darkened human hearts (also known as the noetic effects of sin) so that on our own we're unable to see "the light of the gospel of the glory of Christ, who is the image of God" (2 Corinthians 4:4). Yet—praise the Lord!—he calls the elect to "be conformed to the image of his Son," a process that occurs "from one degree of glory to another" (Romans 8:29; 2 Corinthians 3:18).

The renewal of the *imago Dei* is not only a statement of fact but also a command.[15] Christians are exhorted to "put on the Lord Jesus Christ, and make no provision for the flesh" (Romans 13:14). Therefore, while on the one hand as followers of Christ we *are* the image of Christ, on the other hand we're exhorted to *be* the image of Christ.

In *The Cost of Discipleship,* German pastor and martyred anti-Hitler dissident Dietrich Bonhoeffer discusses what being like Christ means: "When a man follows Jesus Christ and bears the image of the incarnate, crucified, and risen Lord, when he has become the image of God, we may at last say that he has been called to be the 'imitator of God.' The follower of Jesus is the imitator of God."[16]

How do we best imitate God? Puritan John Owen teaches that we're most like God when we love his Son.[17] Because the image of God is his Son, the only correct anthropology is one whose end is Christ.

While the doctrine of the image of God is essential to understanding who we are, it must always be coupled with the fall of Adam and Eve and the doctrine of sin—which is our next focus.

4

THE IMPRINT OF SIN

The Gravity of the Fall

The first time I read the Bible, I was in the Atlanta City Detention Center as an inmate in federal custody. There was no virtuous or spiritual intent behind my reading it; I simply had nothing better to do. I could never have imagined how it would affect me.

It was the day before I was sentenced. I read Psalm 51, and David's words of contrition were *my* words: "Have mercy on me, O God. . . . Against you, you only, have I sinned. . . . Behold, I was brought forth in iniquity" (verses 1, 4–5). I read these words and wept, realizing I'd broken God's law and rebelled against my Creator.

Sometime later, I read Romans 1. In Paul's list of sins, what hit me hardest, oddly enough, was "disobedient to parents" (verse 30). The only people who really loved me unconditionally were my parents, and I had spurned their love in the most dramatic ways imaginable. It broke me to think about the depth of my rebellion in which I so drastically, heartlessly, and selfishly disobeyed them. I certainly *was* a sinner.

During my first couple of months of incarceration, I read about the wickedness of my heart: "For from within, out of the heart of man, come evil thoughts, sexual immorality, theft, murder, adultery, coveting, wickedness, deceit, sensuality, envy, slander, pride, foolishness" (Mark 7:21–22).

But it wasn't just a heart problem. My head was messed up too. I was futile minded and darkened in my understanding (Ephesians 4:17–18). Even my unchosen feelings and thoughts were distorted by sin. God was removing blinders from my eyes so I could see who I really was—who I really am—a sinner. This was not good news.

Years earlier, in boot camp, recruits like myself learned about the history of the United States Marine Corps, including the Battle of Iwo Jima. It was one of the fiercest and bloodiest battles of World War II, with more than twenty Medals of Honor awarded to Marines, many posthumously. One Medal of Honor was given to Private First Class Jack Lucas, who jumped on not one but two grenades and amazingly survived. When asked why he did it, Jack's reply was simple: "I did it to save my buddies."

We extol those who sacrifice their lives for friend and country. But how many men at the Battle of Iwo Jima fell on a grenade to save the lives of their enemies? Not one. Yet God died for us while we were his enemies (Romans 5:6–10). It's one thing for a good man to die for his friend; it's a completely different story for a perfect man to die for his enemy that he might live.

Almost everyone I know enthusiastically embraces God's love. But we cannot grasp the depth of this love without first understanding our own sinfulness. Without knowledge of our total depravity, we cheapen God's love and spit on his grace.

I sign off my emails and letters with the tagline "Undeserving of his grace." In no way do I mean to diminish the fact that Christ's righteousness has been credited to me by faith and I am a sanctified saint (1 Corinthians 1:2), nor am I nullifying the fact that I'm created in God's image. But apart from God, I *am* a sinner—as you are, as all of us are. My signature reminds me that I'm a sinner and that I live by grace alone—*sola gratia*.

This *is* good news.

Again, Back to the Beginning

The doctrine of sin is an essential tenet of Christianity and an integral aspect of God's grand story—creation, fall, redemption, and consummation. All humanity has descended from Adam and Eve, who introduced sin into the world. Consequently, all humans are guilty of Adam's first sin, possess the condition of original sin, and are in desperate need of salvation.

Why is this so important? Because dismissing it is tantamount to rejecting Christ's work on the cross. As theologian John Frame writes, "If we abandon the Christian belief that we fell in Adam, by what right do we maintain that we are saved in Christ?"[1] If Adam neither sinned nor passed along his sinful nature to humankind, there's no need for salvation.

To better understand humanity—and particularly human sexuality—we must again go back to the beginning. After God created Adam and Eve, they at first obeyed God perfectly. Thomas Boston, an eighteenth-century Scottish theologian, calls this the state of innocence.[2]

You know the story. In the Garden of Eden, God permitted them to eat of any tree while also telling them, "Of the tree of the knowledge of good and evil you shall not eat" (Genesis 2:17). In Genesis 3, Adam and Eve disobeyed God and fell into sin by eating the forbidden fruit.

Had God set them up for failure and caused them to sin? Of course not! Scripture informs us that "he himself tempts no one" (James 1:13). In reality, God put the tree in the garden out of his love for Adam and Eve and for their own good. It served as a reminder that, though they were called to rule and have dominion over creation, God still ruled over them. The tree served as a memorial that they could freely choose obedience or disobedience.[3]

After eating of the tree of the knowledge of good and evil, Adam and Eve hid in fear and shame. They shifted blame away from themselves, further confirming their loss of innocence. Their pathetic display of self-ishness stands in sharp contrast to the selflessness of the second Adam, Jesus Christ, who bore our sins and even became sin for us (2 Corinthians 5:21; 1 Peter 2:24). His death on the cross that brought us justification was the antithesis of Adam's self-justification in the garden.

But with Adam's sin established, what does this mean for us today? What are the lasting consequences of the Fall in Genesis 3?

The Fallout

Adam and Eve's sin brought several consequences, death being one of the most obvious. When God warned them not to eat the fruit of this one tree, he added, "For in the day that you eat of it you shall surely die" (Genesis 2:17). In Hebrew, this is an emphatic pronouncement—literally, "dying you shall die."[4] God's firm and absolute decree communicated that the consequence of their disobedience would, without doubt, be death.

This death was both physical—"to dust you shall return" (3:19)—and spiritual, as evidenced by Adam and Eve's separation from God after their expulsion from Eden (verses 23–24). God's punishment also included the curse of pain and turmoil (verses 16–19): "in pain" the woman would bear children, and "in pain" the man would wring out his sustenance by working the cursed ground.

Embedded in this painful judgment, God incorporated a glimmer of hope. In Genesis 3:15, a promise is given that the woman's "offspring" would one day bruise the head of the serpent. This offspring is Jesus Christ, who will be victorious over Satan, sin, and death. This verse is the first messianic prophecy in the Old Testament and the earliest announcement of the good news of the gospel, the protevangelium.

The fallout of Adam and Eve's disobedience has been profound for all humanity—and even for all creation. Paul tells us in Romans that "the creation was subjected to futility" (8:20) and that "because of one man's trespass, death reigned through that one man" (5:17). In 1 Corinthians 15:22, Paul states, "In Adam all die."

The Fall resulted in death, and along with death came other natural consequences—for example, cancer, Alzheimer's, diabetes, pneumonia, and cardiac arrest. Physical and mental disorders, defects, and disabilities —such as blindness, deafness, learning disabilities, Down syndrome, and autism—are also consequences of the Fall. Another example is the biological anomaly known as intersexuality, in which a person's sexual organs don't fit the typical definitions for male or female bodies. Although all these natural conditions are unfortunate and sometimes tragic consequences of the Fall, they are not sinful. The image of God has only been distorted, not lost.

This certainly doesn't sound like good news—but it gets worse. Adam's sin also brought guilt. In modern parlance, guilt is a subjective experience—the *feeling* of having done wrong. But the New Testament concept of guilt has little to do with emotion. It's a judicial concept involving our state of having violated the law and of being liable for punishment.[5]

This is why the orthodox doctrine of sin is so offensive to many. It's difficult to accept that a person is guilty for something he or she didn't do. Being held accountable for Adam's sin seems unjust. However, let's admit that what we think is fair may not be truly fair by God's perfect standards.

We must therefore look to Jesus for a clear understanding of the biblical concept of guilt. In fact, it's impossible to grasp the transmission of Adam's guilt apart from the transmission of Christ's righteousness. The two go hand in hand. "For as in Adam all die," Paul tells us, "so also in Christ shall all be made alive" (1 Corinthians 15:22). Therefore, just as much as the real, historical Jesus is our representative in life, the real, historical Adam is our representative in death.

Paul further explains this in Romans 5:17–19. "For as by the one man's disobedience the many were made sinners, so by the one man's obedience the many will be made righteous" (verse 19). By Adam's act of disobedience, we are sinners; by Christ's act of obedience, we can be made righteous.

If we don't believe Adam's guilt was ascribed to us, we have no basis to believe we're made righteous in Christ. Adam's imputed guilt and Christ's imputed righteousness—it's all or none. In fact, our being guilty of Adam's sin is no more unjust than our being made righteous via Christ's death on the cross!

Original Sin: Our Nature Polluted

Another important moral and ethical consequence of the Fall bears significantly on our understanding of human sexuality. Paul speaks of how "all, both Jews and Greeks, are under sin" (Romans 3:9). Every person is conceived in sin, as David personally confesses in Psalm 51:5. This fallout of Adam's sin passes down indiscriminately to every person so that we're all "by nature children of wrath, like the rest of mankind" (Ephesians 2:3). This key theological concept is called *original sin*.

Like the word *trinity*, the phrase *original sin* isn't found in the Bible, but the concept assuredly is. Many confuse original sin with the first actual sin of Adam and Eve in the garden, but it's not the same. Rather, original sin is the *result* of that first sin, a consequence with extensive moral ramifications.[6] Regrettably, every human being is born with this sinful condition.[7] Taken for what it is, it's the first and greatest equalizer humanity has ever known. We all start off with original sin.

It's called "original" because its origin is from the beginning, and all our *actual* sins—sinful thoughts, desires, words, and actions—originate from it. As Augustine said, original sin is both the daughter and the mother of sin.[8] Why is original sin so important as an essential Christian doctrine? Because only when we understand the pervasiveness of original sin can we fully grasp the immensity of our utter need for rebirth, redemption, and renewal in Christ.

Original sin is the sinful state and condition in which every person is born. In other words, we have a polluted nature. While guilt is a legal status of culpability, original sin is a moral condition. It means that our nature has been corrupted by sin, a condition that produces only more sin.

This corruption is pervasive, impacting the entire human race. "None is righteous, no, not one" (Romans 3:10). This corruption is also pervasive in affecting the entire person. For each of us, sin affects all our faculties: actions, words, thoughts, and desires—including our sexual desires.

However, this does not mean that original sin is an actual substance inside us or one particular aspect of our essence.[9] Rather, it's a pollution and corruption of our full nature and therefore a distortion of God's image. Sin has changed our overall direction from obedience to rebellion. Original sin is not *who* we are but rather a pervasive pollution of our essential identity—in other words, it's *how* we are.

This doesn't mean that we'll all be as wicked as utterly possible or that nothing good remains in us. God's common grace is bestowed on all, saved and unsaved. Unconverted people are certainly capable of doing good things, but even the most altruistic act is tarnished with egocentrism. Every human aspect has in some way, great or small, been blighted by sin.

Sin affects our actions to the extent that Paul can say, "No one does good, not even one" (Romans 3:12, quoting Psalm 14:3). Our words have likewise been perverted, as our mouths are "full of curses and bitterness"

(Romans 3:14; Psalm 10:7). Even our reason and thoughts are tainted, since all people "are darkened in their understanding" (Ephesians 4:18).

Not surprisingly, the desires of our hearts are corrupted as well, as Jesus makes clear: "For from within, out of the heart of man, come evil thoughts, sexual immorality, theft, murder, adultery, coveting, wickedness, deceit, sensuality, envy, slander, pride, foolishness" (Mark 7:21–22).

This pervasive nature of sin is certainly true for unbelievers, but what about those who've been born again and are no longer in bondage to sin? In Galatians 5:16–17, Paul exhorts Christians, "Walk by the Spirit, and you will not gratify the desires of the flesh. For the desires of the flesh are against the Spirit, and the desires of the Spirit are against the flesh, for these are opposed to each other, to keep you from doing the things you want to do." This struggle is not uncommon for the individual postconversion.

Flesh is a term that is distinctly, but not uniquely, Pauline. Although some translations have rendered *flesh* as "sin nature," it should not be mistaken for *who we are* but rather as our fallen human condition.[10] In Galatians 5, Paul communicates that the Holy Spirit indwells believers but the present evil age has not yet passed away.

Therefore, as long as we're on this side of glory, the desires of our flesh will be at war with the desires of the Spirit, and vice versa.[11] The believer's struggle to resist sin is real because sin clings so closely (Hebrews 12:1).

John Owen teaches about *indwelling sin,* which is an "operative effective principle" that inclines us continually toward evil even after conversion.[12] Paul tells believers, "If by the Spirit you put to death the deeds of the body, you will live" (Romans 8:13). Mortification of sin is our constant responsibility, and we must always be vigilant. As Owen was known to say, "Be killing sin or it will be killing you."[13]

Earlier we observed in the garden how Adam and Eve were at first capable of *not* sinning. To use Augustine's Latin phrases, Adam and Eve were both "able not to sin" (*posse non peccare*) and "able to sin" (*posse peccare*).[14] Ever since the Fall—because of the pervasive pollution of sin—unregenerate men and women are "unable not to sin" (*non posse non peccare*).

But an essential aspect of God's grand story is redemption, and as such, born-again believers are now "able not to sin" (*posse non peccare*). Unfortunately, sin persists even in the believer and won't be completely eradicated until the culmination of redemptive history, when God's faithful elect reach glorification on the last day of consummation and are perfectly "unable to sin" (*non posse peccare*).

Like the image of God, original sin is a crucial concept for correctly understanding humanity. But how do these doctrines specifically relate to my gay loved one? Or how do these theological paradigms help me better minister to Christians with same-sex attractions?

In the following chapter, I will make the case that without a correct theological anthropology as the bedrock of our understanding of human sexuality, we are more easily led to subtle but consequential distortions of truth.

5

WHY ANTHROPOLOGY MATTERS

Consequences of Ignoring Who We Are

The Tower of Pisa is known around the world for its unintentional tilt. This freestanding bell tower was built in the twelfth century. Unfortunately, the project was flawed from the beginning: the foundation was a mere three meters, and the subsoil was weak and unstable.

As soon as the construction progressed to the second floor, the building began to sink on one side because the ground was too soft. At its worst, the tower leaned a precarious five and a half degrees. In the 1990s, engineers feared that the tower would collapse. After straightening the tower by one and a half degrees, or forty-five centimeters, the structure was steadied . . . but only temporarily.[1]

In the conversation on sexuality, beginning with the correct foundation is of ultimate importance. When I was a kid, my mother taught me a well-known Chinese proverb: *Chā zhī háo lí, shī zhī qiān lǐ,* which translates as "A millimeter discrepancy leads to a thousand-mile loss." If the point of departure is a bit off from the start, the deviation in the end can be overwhelmingly large.

When it comes to sexuality, the place to start must always be the image of God and the doctrine of sin. No Christian should ever challenge these fundamental principles. But when addressing sexuality, I believe some suffer from amnesia regarding a biblical understanding of who we are. This mistake leads to conclusions that seem a thousand miles away from truth.

Allow me to explain with a few examples.

Arrogant Condemnation

My perception as a gay man, before I came to Christ, was that Christians thought gays and lesbians deserved a hotter place in hell and that Jesus had to hang on the cross a little longer for the sin of same-sex relationships. Many non-Christians have the impression that followers of Jesus view same-sex relationships as the worst sin possible. But Scripture says there's only one unforgivable sin: blaspheming the Holy Spirit, not homosexual behavior (Matthew 12:31–32; Mark 3:28–29; Luke 12:10).

To that point, one time after speaking at a church near a military base, I was approached by an older gentleman who told me he was a Vietnam veteran. He'd attended all my talks from the Sunday service and even returned that evening. Prior to that morning, he hadn't planned to come to any of my talks; in fact, he was upset that the church was even spending time on this topic. "What else needs to be said? It's sin!"

But during the service, when he heard my parents' testimony and their love for their gay son, he was "punched in the gut" by the Holy Spirit. He told me that when he was younger, if he'd known another soldier was gay, he would have shot him in the back during combat—all while claiming to be a Christian.

His voice wavered, and his eyes welled up with tears as he said, "Today I realize I'm wrong. Will you forgive me?" I'll never forget that emotional moment as he hugged me and wept on my shoulder. Paul tells us in Romans 2:4, "God's kindness is meant to lead you to repentance."

To begin this journey on the right foot, we must each humbly recognize and repent of our own sinfulness.

Paul knew that he was the foremost of sinners, yet God used him "as an example to those who were to believe in him for eternal life" (1 Timothy 1:16). And more importantly, even the sinner guilty of the most heinous crimes is still created in God's image. The more we realize how sinful we are, the humbler we should become, and the more God can use us as an example of the gospel.

Should we warn others of the dangers of sin? Of course we should! But how are we doing it? It's been said about the great nineteenth-century evangelist Dwight Lyman Moody that he was most qualified to preach about hell and the wrath of God because he did it with tears.

Humility is a great place to start, especially when our goal is to point people to Christ. I've yet to meet anyone who was introduced to Jesus by someone who acted holier than thou! Only when we view ourselves as sinners are we able to see other sinners as God does.

Incorrect Diagnosis

One of the unfortunate consequences of having a lowered immune system from HIV is that I'm more prone to getting sick than the average person. When I'm not feeling well, the first thing I want is an accurate medical diagnosis of my ailment. A correct diagnosis means correct treatment, while an incorrect diagnosis means incorrect treatment. Discerning the root of the problem is the key to a proper response. The same process applies to all aspects of the human condition.

Unfortunately, homosexuality has been diagnosed incorrectly for decades. You've most likely heard it said that homosexuality's primary root causes are an absentee father, dominant mother, or past trauma. In other words, a deficient and imperfect childhood is the culprit behind same-sex attractions.

My older brother and I had very similar upbringings, yet he never struggled with same-sex attractions. I was also never sexually abused; however, same-sex attraction is a part of my reality. Many individuals seem to have near-perfect Christian upbringings but still experience unwanted same-sex attractions.

Christians seem to have blindly accepted these supposed root causes with little critical and biblical reflection. Often the studies mentioned to support these claims show some correlation, but correlation doesn't constitute causation. Certainly, parents can have positive and negative influences on their children, but influence is not the same as cause. Abuse has grave effects on an individual, but a detrimental life event is not the root for anyone's struggle with sin.

To be honest, I know of no other sin struggle where the blame is placed squarely on the shoulders of parents. The last thing hurting parents need is to be wrongfully accused of causing their children's same-sex attractions. The diagnosis that homosexuality is a psychological and developmental disorder induced by bad parenting doesn't line up with Scripture at all. It's more Freudian than biblical. We struggle with sin not because we had an imperfect upbringing but simply because we're sinners.

For any other sin, Christians recognize that original sin is behind it. But for homosexuality, they seem to make a special exception, saying same-sex attractions are primarily a result of one's upbringing and not the Fall. Yet if our environment causes us to sin, then there's no need for Jesus—all we need is a better environment. His death on the cross is then insufficient, and justification and sanctification depend on human effort. We're not quibbling about different opinions here; the sufficiency of Christ is on the line, which is no insignificant matter.

For those of you parents who are weighed down with guilt and wondering, *What did I do wrong?* or *How could I have prevented this?* Please listen to me: It's not your fault. Sure, parents should hope to influence their children for better and not for worse. But perfect parenting does not guarantee perfect children. Look at Adam and Eve. They had a perfect Father and were raised in a perfect environment, yet they still rebelled! What makes us think we can do any better?

When it comes down to it, the primary goal of Christian parenting is not necessarily to *produce* godly children but, first and foremost, to *be* godly parents. Parents, you are not God! The gifts of faith, sanctification, and eternal life are not for parents to grant—only God revives and redeems.

When we rightly remember the biblical doctrine of sin, we realize that any sin (such as same-sex sexual practice) or any struggle with sin (such as resisting same-sex sexual desire) has only one root cause: original sin. Things from our past are secondary catalysts, not the primary source. This is not a novel idea; it's simply orthodoxy. Furthermore, there's no biblical evidence that developmental psychotherapy will resolve or diminish our sinful temptations.

In the fourth and fifth centuries, Pelagius was an ascetic who practiced rigid moralism. He opposed Augustine's theory of original sin and taught that Adam's sin had zero impact on the rest of humanity. The church's Council of Carthage in AD 418 condemned Pelagius and his perspectives on sin and humanity as heretical.

Original sin is essential to a biblical understanding of justification, and rejecting it places one outside of orthodoxy. However, the foundation of many ideas floating around pop Christianity bear more resemblance to Pelagianism than biblical truth. In essence, to claim that the primary root of homosexuality is anything but original sin is to deny orthodoxy.

Furthermore, this has immobilized many pastors with the lie that without professional training they cannot help a same-sex-attracted individual. Certainly, pastors must strive to be better informed, and biblical counseling is beneficial. But it's sad and troublesome when the only pastoral response to same-sex attractions is a referral. Every pastor should know how to minister to someone struggling with sin.

Same-sex attraction finds its root in original sin and as such is not really that exceptional. Every one of us has sinful distortions of our sexuality. Homosexuality is often called abnormal, but the stark reality is that, for some, it actually *feels* quite normal and even natural.

As a matter of fact, sin in general feels normal and natural to all of us, which is what makes it so enticing, addictive, and deceptive. What is *not* normal is putting to death the sin that dwells within us (Romans 7:23; 8:13). All sinful temptations and behavior present us with a real struggle and fight.

You may ask, "How can I help someone with same-sex attractions when I don't personally struggle with it?" Then answer this: Since when do we have to struggle with a specific sin before we can help another with that same sin? Do I have to commit adultery before I can minister to an adulterer? Do I have to dabble in pornography before I can assist a porn addict? Do I need to gossip before I can aid a gossiper? If you know Jesus and have had some victory over sin, you can be of help to another sinner.

Homosexuality isn't a psychological disorder or a developmental problem. To think that way is a futile, human-centered attempt to erase the reality of original sin. Let's call sin what it is. When we do, we realize that the answer is not human-centered; the only answer for sin is Jesus Christ. Sin is the great problem; Jesus is the great solution.

Categorical Error

Our amnesia toward original sin doesn't express itself just in a wrong diagnosis. It also occurs when the concept of sin is replaced with a seemingly innocuous, more tolerable and acceptable category: sexual orientation.

It's no surprise that the secular world tries to sanitize and erase sin. But when Christians view a homosexual orientation as neutral and innocent—simply an unchosen and persistent phenomenological pattern of same-sex attractions—could we be turning a blind eye to the doctrine of sin?

It's untrue that Christians with same-sex attractions have only two options: either be ex-gay or be celibate. I believe that both these paths fall short in the same way—by elevating sexual orientation as a redeemable category.

"Ex-gays" contend that sexual orientation can change from homosexual to heterosexual, even if only in slight, gradual ways. "Gay celibate Christians" contend that sexual orientation cannot change, that the only option is lifelong celibacy. Thus, one side elevates opposite-sex sexual orientation as ideal, and the other elevates same-sex sexual orientation as sanctifiable. Both rely on a wrong framework.

When there's a choice between a biblical framework and a secular framework, Christians should favor the biblical over the secular. In regard to understanding the capacity to experience same-sex attractions—unchosen and persistent sexual and romantic desires toward the same sex—is there a biblical framework that's better than the secular concept of sexual orientation?

Yes, there is. That framework is *sin*.

I'm not saying the *capacity* to have same-sex attractions or temptations is *actual* sin. However, the concept of original and indwelling sin fits every description of a same-sex sexual orientation. Original sin is an unchosen condition, and indwelling sin is a persistent pattern of sinful desires or behaviors. Shouldn't we therefore choose biblical terminology over secular? Why try to reappropriate and redeem a term when a working biblical framework already exists?

Some say that sexual and romantic attractions to people of the same sex are rooted in the image of God, not in the Fall, and that they are therefore good or even sanctifiable. However, if same-sex sexual behavior is sinful, then its desire is rooted in the Fall, not in the image of God.

We must, however, go further than saying that erotic and romantic same-sex attractions are simply a consequence of the Fall. We must ask whether they are a *natural* consequence or a *moral* consequence. As we discussed in the previous chapter, an example of a natural consequence of the Fall is disease or physical disability, like cancer or blindness. Natural consequences are not immoral.

If same-sex sexual attractions were only a natural consequence of the Fall, then they would be neutral—and, as some assert, potentially sanctifiable. However, if *acting* on same-sex attractions is sin, then there's nothing neutral or sanctifiable about it. Sexual sin always involves a moral component. Same-sex attraction finds its genesis in original sin. And let's be crystal clear: there's *nothing* neutral or innocent about original sin.

This is a categorical error. The secular concept of sexual orientation does not fit into the biblical framework regarding sexual morality. Distinguishing between what's right and what's wrong becomes difficult, especially since not all opposite-sex sexual desires and relationships are right. If, however, we construct the category for thinking about sexuality biblically around both the concept of *imago Dei* and the doctrine of sin, then discerning what's right and what's wrong becomes much clearer. We will flesh out and explain this biblical category in the next chapter.

With same-sex attractions, the problem is sin, and the gospel is the answer.

Born That Way

But aren't people born gay? According to media and pop culture, this seems to be a fact that science has unquestionably proven. Of the numerous studies conducted to investigate the potential biological and environmental factors that may influence the development of same-sex attractions, nothing yet has been conclusive.

The American Psychiatric Association recently made this statement: "Some people believe that sexual orientation is innate and fixed; however, sexual orientation develops across a person's lifetime."[2] Scientists are far from discovering the factors that contribute to the development of sexual attractions, so it's untenable and irresponsible to claim that the innateness of sexual attractions is a proven reality.

Despite a lack of evidence, the belief persists that people are born gay and thus many conclude that same-sex sexual behavior is no less immoral than eye color. Yet innateness doesn't mean something is permissible, for being born a sinner doesn't make sin right. We must point people to a far more important claim the Bible makes: regardless of what was true or not true when you were born, Jesus says, "You must be born again" (John 3:7)

It doesn't matter whether you think you were born an alcoholic; you must be born again. It doesn't matter whether you think you were born a liar; you must be born again. It doesn't matter whether you think you were born a porn addict; you must be born again. It doesn't matter whether you think you were born with any other sexual sin struggle; you must be born again.

When we're born again, the old has gone, and the new has come—we are a new creation (2 Corinthians 5:17). We're able to hate our sin without hating ourselves. Our sexuality is no longer *who* we are but *how* we are. We put to death our old self so that Christ can live in us (Galatians 2:20). The effect of sin is so pervasive, so complete, so radical that complete rebirth must occur for anyone to enter the kingdom of heaven (John 3:3).

Whatever our condition upon coming into the world, we need a total transformation—the kind that our God and Creator has made inexplicably possible only by grace through faith in Christ. This isn't a message just for the gay community or only for those who experience same-sex attractions. This is a message for everybody: *you must be born again*.

This is good news.

6

HOLY SEXUALITY

God's Good Intent for All

Over the last few years, my dad, mom, and I have had the privilege of getting to know numerous fathers and mothers with children identifying as gay or lesbian. We've been able to personally walk with several of these parents through difficult stages of their journey. For many, it's been a long and emotional ride. I'll never forget meeting one particular mother.

As she approached, the look on her face revealed that it took all her strength to keep it together. She stepped toward me and lowered her head into her hands. The dam broke, and the tears flowed as she released her pent-up emotions. I put my hand on her shoulder and said softly, "It's okay. It's okay."

She tried to get out the words she'd come to say but couldn't stop weeping. I offered a few more words of comfort to fill the void, telling her I had all the time she needed. After a few moments, she was able to put together a sentence. "I just . . . just want my son . . . to be normal."

Normal.

Through sobs, this devastated mother recounted that her son had told her he was gay and was moving in with his boyfriend. She was crushed and hadn't told anyone, including her husband. She continued to express deep disappointment, wondering why this son couldn't be like her other son—*normal*—with a steady girlfriend and even a baby on the way.

Somehow this mother's moral compass had been thrown off. She failed to realize that her idea of right was actually wrong. In her view, her gay son was not okay, while her fornicating one was fine. Like many today, this grieving mother wrongly equated normal—that is, all forms of heterosexuality, including extramarital relationships—with moral and good. I know some of you may be thinking right now, *But heterosexuality is ordained by God!* Stay with me and hear me out. This may be one of the most important points of the book.

Without doubt, same-sex relationships are sinful. But does this mean that heterosexuality—*in all its forms*—is blessed by God? Many assume it is. For decades, the aim of some "Christian" counseling for those with unwanted same-sex attractions has been to develop "heterosexual potential."[1]

However, does the Bible truly promote and wholly bless heterosexuality *in all its forms*? Heterosexuality constitutes the correct general direction, but does it adequately and fully describe how we all should behave sexually? What about unmarried people? How about those not in any relationship?

What is the biblical standard for sexuality? Does heterosexuality accurately and comprehensively describe sexual morality for everyone married and single? As evangelicals, our benchmark is Scripture, and everything must be measured to it.

Time to Break Free

To begin, we must define *sexuality.* According to the *New Shorter Oxford English Dictionary on Historical Principles,* sexuality consists of different aspects: sexual expression, sexual desires, and a capacity for sexual desires.[2] Since actions are more concrete and easier to assess than desires, we'll start there and then, in the following three chapters, address desires and capacity for desires.

In this chapter, we'll analyze what sexual expression is and whether heterosexuality accurately and comprehensively represents God's perfect and specific standard. If it does not, then we'll seek to find a correct term to fully and unambiguously articulate biblical sexuality. Once we're able to establish the criteria for sexual behavior, we'll be better positioned to evaluate the other two aspects of desires and capacity for desires.

To aid in our assessment, here's a definition for *heterosexual:* "pertaining to sexual relations between people of opposite sex."[3] This is exceedingly broad and would include behavior the Bible deems sinful—for example, a man sleeping with several different women, a husband cheating on his wife with another lady, and even a committed monogamous relationship between a cohabitating boyfriend and girlfriend. Today, these three scenarios of heterosexuality may be common and normal but are without question sinful in God's eyes.

Yet some Christians would actually consider these "success" stories for same-sex-attracted individuals who have achieved their "heterosexual potential." The Bible does not bless every indiscriminate variety of opposite-sex relationship. God declares that only sex between a husband and a wife in marriage is good. Every sexual expression outside this context—whether in an opposite-sex relationship or a same-sex relationship—God condemns as sinful.

Here are a few biblical examples of sinful sexual relationships that would be defined as heterosexual. In the Old Testament, we read about the incest of Lot's daughters with their father (Genesis 19:31–36), the rape of Dinah by Shechem (Genesis 34:2), the fornication of Samson and the prostitute (Judges 16:1), the adultery of David and Bathsheba (2 Samuel 11:1–5), the incestuous rape of Tamar by Amnon (2 Samuel 13:1–19), and the harlotry of Gomer, Hosea's wife (Hosea 3:1–3).

In the New Testament, we are told about the incest and adultery of Herod (Matthew 14:3–4; Mark 6:17–18; Luke 3:19), the prodigal son with prostitutes (Luke 15:30), the unmarried Samaritan woman living with the sixth in a series of men (John 4:16–18), and the church in Corinth's boasting about a man who "has his father's wife" (1 Corinthians 5:1). The New Testament mentions adultery (Greek *moicheia* with its four other forms) thirty-two times and sexual immorality (*porneia* with its three other forms) fifty-five times—and these mainly refer to heterosexual sin.

By simply stating that "heterosexuality is right" without qualification, we imply a tacit endorsement of all the sexual immorality listed above. Certainly, not all heterosexual behavior or relationships are sinful—the union between a husband and a wife is blessed by God—but we must also recognize that heterosexuality is *not* synonymous with biblical marriage. This is the bottom line: By broadly affirming heterosexuality, we also, whether inadvertently or not, endorse heterosexual sin.

As I discussed in my chapter on identity, the terms *heterosexual* and *homosexual* originate from a secular anthropology that elevates sexual desires as a legitimate way to categorize humanity. Is this really an ontological category Christians should espouse? Are we in fact defined by our sexual desires and behaviors?

The world espouses these terms, *heterosexuality* and *homosexuality*, in part because sexual desires and sexual expression are of utmost importance to them. It's trumpeted in our classrooms and on our television screens that sex and sexuality are inseparable, necessary, and essential aspects of who we are.

Borrowing this secular, human-made category of heterosexuality to

describe how Christians must live misses God's perfect standard for sexual expression. The Bible does not categorize humanity according to our
sexual desires—or any other sort of desire.

We live in a new world that not only embraces same-sex marriage as
legitimate but also conflates heterosexuality and homosexuality with who
we are. Using a term that confuses our true identity is unwise, and embracing such a broad category that includes sinful behavior should be
roundly rejected. In our culture of confusion, ambiguity is no longer an
option. Instead of affirming what's generally normal, common, or usual,
we must look precisely at what's *biblical*.

But what other options do we have, you may ask, other than heterosexuality and homosexuality? What we need is a completely new paradigm to represent God's sexual ethic.

Holy sexuality.

We've pigeonholed ourselves into the wrong framework for biblical
sexual expression: heterosexuality, bisexuality, or homosexuality. It's time
to break free from this paradigm and embrace God's vision for sexuality.
Holy sexuality consists of two paths: chastity in singleness and faithfulness in marriage. Chastity is more than simply abstention from extramarital sex; it conveys purity and holiness. Faithfulness is more than
merely maintaining chastity and avoiding illicit sex; it conveys covenantal commitment.

Both of these embody the *only* correct biblical sexual ethic and unambiguously articulate the exact expressions of sexual behavior that God
blesses. Too often Christians focus only on marriage but forget about
singleness. Case in point—heterosexuality says nothing about chastity in
singleness. Yet God blesses both biblical marriage and singleness; one
without the other doesn't sufficiently describe God's will. In a world that
blurs the lines of morality into every shade of gray, we must realize that
biblical sexuality is more black and white than we think.

To be honest, I'm really not presenting anything new or monumental. From Genesis to Revelation, in the entirety of the biblical witness, only two paths align with God's standard for sexual expression: if you're single, be sexually abstinent while fleeing lustful desires; if you're married, be sexually and emotionally faithful to your spouse of the opposite sex while also fleeing lustful desires.

No terminology has accurately represented the biblical standard for sexual expression, which encompasses these two ways of living. While the category of heterosexuality includes some sinful behavior, it also does not clearly include chaste singleness. Therefore, a new phrase is necessary— *holy sexuality.* The purpose of this phrase is to transcend the current secular paradigm of sexual orientation that is unable to point toward God's clear intent for sexual expression.

This term *holy sexuality* is meant to simplify and disentangle the complex and confusing conversation around sexuality. The truth is that God's standard for *everyone* is holy sexuality: chastity in singleness and faithfulness in marriage. Different expectations for different people are not only unfair; they're unbiblical. Instead of determining how we ought to live based on enduring patterns of erotic desires, God's call for *all* humanity, quite simply, is holiness.

The argument against same-sex relationships has often been primarily or exclusively an appeal to natural design. Sometimes Scripture is only tangentially mentioned. This prioritizes general revelation (nature) above special revelation (Scripture). Both are important; however, natural design has its limitations to fully and accurately communicate biblical sexuality.

Natural design points only to opposite-sex sexual intimacy—in other words, heterosexuality *in all its forms.* Thus, a natural design argument on its own obscures heterosexual sin. It's Scripture that specifically points to one man and one woman in marriage or to chaste singleness, which is why holy sexuality is an exact and full explanation for a biblical sexual ethic.

The inspired and inerrant Word of God defines marriage as a holy covenant between a husband and wife before God. The world has rejected this definition and made up a new one. The *Oxford English Dictionary* defines marriage as "the legally or formally recognized union of two people as partners in a personal relationship."[4]

Therefore, to affirm the correct, biblical definition of marriage, I will use the phrase *biblical marriage* and sometimes, for the sake of brevity, *marriage*. To refer to the incorrect and unbiblical form, I will always use a modifier—*same-sex marriage*.

Holy sexuality is chastity in singleness and faithfulness in marriage. Notice that I'm careful to describe these as two paths, not "choices." Singleness for most is *not* a choice. If you think about it, no one is born married—we're all born single! Singleness is default. While a few may choose to *remain* single, it's never initially our own choice. Ultimately, some of these difficult paths are determined by our sovereign God.

At thirty-three, Bill became a Christian after being in and out of same-sex relationships for eleven years. He had a desire to marry and have children. However, thirty years later, he remains unmarried and perseveres in the midst of his same-sex attractions. Now sixty-three, he has been able to find contentment in his singleness. Bill leads a full life and mentors many men with similar experiences as himself. He also realizes that most singles in the church aren't single by choice—whether experiencing same-sex attractions or not.

You may be thinking, then, that lifelong singleness is the only option for same-sex-attracted people. Allow me to recount an interesting story of another friend who thought he had only one option until God did the unexpected.

After years in the gay community, Mark became a Christian and no longer pursued same-sex relationships. He never had interest in women even as a new believer. With a close network of friends from his new family, the church, he was content to be single for the rest of his life—assuming it was his only option.

Mark had a close friend, Andrea, who was also a new follower of Christ. She came out of a broken past that consisted of abusive boyfriends and a few abortions. Because of her past toxic relationships, she'd decided to hold off on dating to focus on her relationship with God.

The two felt really safe together. Mark knew she didn't want to date, and Andrea knew he wasn't attracted to girls. He considered her his best friend and most trusted confidante. He loved her like a sister.

After some time, Mark began noticing new things about her. New affections blossomed—both physical and emotional. He jokes now, saying that puberty was hard enough to go through once; try going through puberty twice! He built up enough courage and asked Andrea out on a date.

After several months of dating, he asked her to marry him! And on their wedding night, he confessed to his new bride, "Honey, I cannot explain this. I'm not attracted to any other women. I'm only attracted to you."

In life, God determines what path we'll be on. Bill wanted to marry but remains single today. Mark was content as a single man, but now he's married to Andrea. Sometimes it's not what we expect or even want at the time. For some, it's singleness; for others, it's marriage. And when a man and woman obediently heed God's call to marry each other, God will provide everything those two people need to fulfill their covenant relationship.

Mark may still experience attractions toward the same sex, but God has supernaturally given him emotional, romantic, and sexual affections for Andrea that he never had for any other woman. Who are we to say that the improbable is absolutely impossible?

Sexual Desire in Marriage

Here's something else to think about: Is sexual desire truly a prerequisite for marriage? Is eroticism the litmus test for a godly and healthy cove-nantal union? Or has the sexual revolution influenced us to distort mar-riage into merely the outlet for our sexual appetite and little else?

Actually, we may be guilty of oversexualizing marriage. Let's reevalu-ate the assumption that the absence of sexual passion is often equated with an unhealthy marriage. Consensual sexual intimacy in marriage is good, but I'm not convinced it's the bedrock of a successful marriage. If you ask couples married over fifty years, it's unlikely you'll hear them say that great sex was the defining factor of their love. Is it wrong for sexual desires to develop over time?

Before my conversion, I heard the "Christian" message loud and clear: homosexuality is wrong, and heterosexuality is right. If I wanted to become a Christian, I had to be sexually attracted to women—as if the more erotic desires I had for women, the more of a Christian man I would be. Christians have wrongly assumed—and some still do—that the *main* goal for someone like me is to stop or lessen same-sex attractions and to develop opposite-sex attractions.

You may ask, "What's the harm in that? If a same-sex-attracted indi-vidual wants to marry someone of the opposite sex, wouldn't developing heterosexual attractions help achieve that goal?" But by making sexual desire the main objective, we could end up going from one gutter to an-other. Let me relate to you this real story as an illustration.

A pastor I met had a friend with same-sex attractions who was going through orientation-change counseling. One day while driving down the highway and passing a billboard for a local strip club, his friend noted how the scantily clad female model looked "hot."

The pastor was taken aback and even explained that in any other circumstance, this would have resulted in a stern rebuke. However, in this case, they actually celebrated what was deemed to be a sign of "success." Like the mother with the gay son, a faulty framework and inaccurate foundation leads to an incorrect conclusion—and in this case, even the celebration and normalization of sin.

So how do I best help someone who desires to marry? Point that person to Christ. Help him be a more godly man. Help her be a more godly woman. The key to a successful marriage is not sexual desires but union with Christ. And even with heterosexual feelings, an individual must continue to resist sinful temptations.

Heterosexuality will not get you into heaven and is not the ultimate goal for those with same-sex attractions. God commands us to "be holy, for I am holy" (Leviticus 11:44–45; 19:2; 20:7; 1 Peter 1:16). Because God is holy, he requires his people to be holy as well.

Thus, the biblical opposite of homosexuality is not heterosexuality—that's not the ultimate goal. But the opposite of homosexuality is holiness. As a matter of fact, the opposite of any sin struggle is holiness!

From God's Word, we see that sexual expression isn't all bad or dirty. It's God's good gift to a husband and a wife to enjoy within the context of marriage. Any sex outside this is not God's will. However, by allowing the orientation paradigm of heterosexuality, bisexuality, and homosexuality to frame the conversation, we're incapable of precisely communicating the correct, biblical modes for sexual expression.

Godly marriage and godly singleness are two sides of the same coin. We should stop emphasizing only one without the other. Both are good. Holy sexuality—chastity in singleness and faithfulness in marriage—is God's good standard for *everyone*.

THE TEMPTATIONS

Addressing Same-Sex Attractions

Same-sex sexual expression is sinful, but what about same-sex attractions? As a new Christian, I had defined attraction to be equivalent to temptation. Therefore, I believed that all same-sex attractions were *not* sinful—because temptations were *not* sinful. However, I realized not everyone defined attraction the same.

Does attraction mean temptation? Does attraction mean desire? Does attraction mean lust? Or is it a combination of these? This is where confusion arises. If we can't even define attraction, how can we assert whether it's sinful or not? *Sin* is a word found throughout the Bible. However, the word *attraction* is not. Instead, the biblical writers use other similar terms like *temptation, desire, covet,* and *lust.*

To avoid further confusion, I'm not going to consider whether same-sex *attractions* are sinful; instead we'll examine whether same-sex *temptations* are sinful and whether same-sex *desires* are sinful. In this chapter we'll first discuss the concept of temptation, and in the following chapter we'll discuss the concepts of desire, covet, and lust.

Tempted in Every Respect

The reality of temptation is found throughout the pages of God's grand story. In Genesis 3, the cunning serpent successfully tempted Adam and

Eve to rebel against God. In the New Testament, we see Satan tempting Jesus in the wilderness. But unlike the first Adam, the second Adam obeyed God perfectly, fully doing the will of God (Matthew 4:1–11; Mark 1:12–13; Luke 4:1–13).

The writer of Hebrews speaks of the real temptations in the life of Jesus: "For we do not have a high priest who is unable to sympathize with our weaknesses, but one who in every respect has been tempted as we are, yet without sin" (Hebrews 4:15). Here in this verse, "our weaknesses" refers to our moral frailty and propensity to sin.[1]

Yet Jesus's sympathy for our weaknesses goes beyond a mere theoretical understanding. He offers actual assistance when we're tempted. "For because he himself has suffered when tempted, he is able to help those who are being tempted" (Hebrews 2:18). The Son of God's sympathy derives from his full participation in humanity and his exposure to the same experiences as the rest of us.

But this doesn't mean Jesus needed to sin in order to sympathize. As the apostle John writes, "You know that he appeared in order to take away sins, and *in him there is no sin*" (1 John 3:5, emphasis added). As God, Jesus did not sin and in fact is incapable of sinning (this is called *impeccability*). Therefore, the temptations of Jesus were not sinful. But then how can he sympathize with our temptations?

Jesus's inability to sin does not diminish in any way the reality of his real and intense struggle with temptation. In fact, his sinlessness in the midst of temptation makes him the ultimate example of struggling— because he never succumbed. Nineteenth-century British theologian B. F. Westcott provides the most lucid explanation of Christ's sympathy:

> The power of sympathy lies not in the mere capacity for feeling,
> but in the lessons of experience. And again, sympathy with the
> sinner in his trial does not depend on the experience of sin but

on the experience of the strength of the temptation to sin which only the sinless can know in its full intensity. He who falls yields before the last strain.[2]

Jesus struggled with temptation infinitely more than any sinful man or woman, yet he was victorious. The Son of Man was tempted in every respect; he *fully* and *perfectly* struggled, bringing his endurance to completion. This should be an extraordinary encouragement for all—particularly those of us who struggle with same-sex attractions.

Yes, our Lord has struggled much *more* than we have. As a matter of fact, because we give in and yield to temptation and sin, we comprehend the struggle only in part. Jesus alone has struggled *wholly,* as he withstood heroically to the end. What an amazing Savior and friend we have in Jesus!

A Way of Escape

Paul reminds us in 1 Corinthians 10 of the tragic example of the Israelites in the wilderness and sternly warns us to flee idolatry and sexual immorality. In the midst of these strong words, he also provides an encouraging and empowering promise: "No temptation has overtaken you that is not common to man. God is faithful, and he will not let you be tempted beyond your ability, but with the temptation he will also provide the way of escape, that you may be able to endure it" (verse 13).

The Greek verb *peirazo* can be translated as "try, test, trap, or tempt."[3] The difference between a test and a temptation lies in the motivation of the tester. For example, God can allow believers to face a trial to test and sharpen their character (John 6:6). On the other hand, Satan tempts people to sin and disobey God (1 Corinthians 7:5).

A test or temptation can build us up or tear us down. Puritan John

Owen explains it best: "Temptation is like a knife, that may either cut the meat or the throat of a man; it may be his food or his poison, his exercise or his destruction."[4]

Sometimes it's obvious whether the test or temptation arises from God, from Satan, from another, or from within. Yet in other instances, the word *peirazo* can generally refer to both test and temptation without excluding either—as it does in 1 Corinthians 10:13.[5]

Paul is reminding us that our trials and temptations aren't exceptional, unique, or even unbearable. Satan wants us to think that no one else can understand our struggles. This is a lie. One of the devil's best weapons is isolation. The truth is that we're *never* alone in our fight.

The comfort of Paul's message in this verse finds its source in three words: "God is faithful." Our confidence in the midst of temptation lies not in our own finite abilities but in a faithful and powerful God who never encounters anything he cannot resolve. God provides assurance that each temptation will be in proportion to the capability of the tempted, along with the promise of a "way of escape."

Please catch what Paul is saying here! Superhuman capacity or even great faith is *not* required to endure temptation. Even the weakest of believers has an escape hatch. This is a comforting salve for the feeble and even for those with little faith. Every temptation always falls within the ability of the one tempted to persevere. The true test may not be in our *ability* to endure temptation but in the depth of our *belief* in the sovereignty of almighty God.

Unfortunately, a serious fallacy runs rampant in our churches that a good Christian is somehow immune to temptation. This simply isn't accurate. Scripture doesn't promise that faith in Jesus results in an eradication of temptations. If Jesus himself was tempted, what makes us think we won't be? The Christian life doesn't mean you won't be tempted; it means you'll have the Spirit-wrought ability to be holy even in the midst of temptations. What matters most is not that we are tempted but how we respond to temptation.

If you're wracked with guilt for simply having same-sex sexual temptations, hear these words from John Owen: "It is impossible that we should be so freed from temptation as not to be at all tempted."[6] Being tempted doesn't mean you have little faith because it's quite ordinary and human to be tempted. The truth of the matter is that temptations are *not* sinful.

However, we must be careful not to take temptation lightly. It is not sin *per se,* but it also isn't benign, as it quickly leads to sin. Therefore, we should always be vigilant in our response to it. *No* temptation to sin is trivial or inconsequential, and that's indeed true for same-sex temptations.

James provides a sober warning that temptation is tantalizing: "Each person is tempted when he is lured and enticed by his own desire. Then desire when it has conceived gives birth to sin, and sin when it is fully grown brings forth death" (James 1:14–15). Although this is not meant to be a step-by-step timeline for sin and temptation, in verse 13 James explains that God does not tempt us to sin and warns us that temptation leads to sin, which leads to death.

There is nothing innocent or sanctifiable about same-sex temptations. They are a stark reality of the distorting effects of original sin. And everyone's sexuality has been distorted by the Fall. Therefore, resisting, fighting, and fleeing temptations must be a vital and normal aspect of a mature Christian's life.

The heart of the matter is not whether we're tempted but how we respond. Do we resist temptation, or do we allow it to turn into sin? It's not a matter of *if* we're tempted but *when.*

But rest assured: Jesus is able to sympathize and help. And God is faithful, apportioning temptation according to our ability to resist while always providing a way out. In our struggles, we are *never* alone.

ANATOMY OF DESIRE

Seeing the End from the Beginning

While in Bible college and seminary, I read about some of the notable church fathers. One especially stood out to me because of his unique conversion story. As a young man, Augustine of Hippo (AD 354–430) was fueled by his carnal desires and lived a life of hedonism and sexual immorality. But God heard the patient and persistent prayers of his devout Christian mother, Monica. It's fascinating how similar my conversion was to his.

Although Augustine rejected the faith in which he was raised and held to various pagan philosophies, he began listening to the sermons of Ambrose, the bishop of Milan. This only added to the mental and emotional strain from battling his fleshly desires. One day in his garden, Augustine was in bitter turmoil and cried out to God, "O Lord, how long?"[1]

As he wept, he heard a child's voice from a neighboring house: "Take up and read." On a nearby table lay some of Paul's epistles that Augustine had been reading, so he picked up and read the nearest text at hand:

Let us walk properly as in the daytime, not in orgies and drunkenness, not in sexual immorality and sensuality, not in quarreling and jealousy. But put on the Lord Jesus Christ, and make no provision for the flesh, to gratify its desires. (Romans 13:13–14)

Augustine later wrote that he immediately felt serenity in his heart after reading these verses. The power of the Word of God penetrated his hardened heart in a remarkable way and brought about a radical transformation. Because of its impact on Augustine, I have put this passage on my bathroom mirror and read it every morning in preparation for my day.

Desire is a key concept in Augustine's writings. We are all created to desire God as our highest good. But because of the corruption of original sin, the object of our desire has shifted away from God. Thus, we now desire what is created rather than the Creator (Romans 1:25). Augustine articulates this best in his famous prayer, "You have made us for Yourself, and our hearts are restless until they rest in You."[2]

Some church fathers seem to conflate human desires with sexual desires. But as we know, not all desire is sexual. In the same way, we shouldn't reduce same-sex desires to eroticism. As a matter of fact, sex is often of minor significance in lesbian relationships and intense romantic desires are the norm.

Yet, while sexuality does consist of *more* than sexual attractions, it definitely is not any *less*. The question is, How much more? Should sexuality be so broadly defined as an affective capacity for relationship to include even a pure, platonic desire for friendship?[3] Should it also include admiration of beauty, as in an aesthetic orientation?[4] If we take these suggestions and widen the meaning of same-sex attractions to this extent, then we've just obliterated the distinction between opposite-sex and same-sex desires. And as a result, everyone now has same-sex attractions!

But if we should not broaden the meaning that far, what types of desires do constitute sexuality? Can we say that same-sex desires in general are *not* sinful? Or maybe more importantly, how do we discern between good desire and bad desire? Is it too burdensome to constantly have to parse out these desires? And ultimately, how are our desires shaped by God's grand story?

Every one of us experiences desires. It may be one of the most intimate and personal realities in our daily lives. Our conclusions regarding the above questions are of great importance and relevance to every Christian. Therefore, let's again look to Scripture for the answers.

Desire in God's Word

In some religious systems, the absence of desire is the ideal state of human existence. However, the Bible communicates no such thing—desire in itself is not bad. We can find several examples of good desire in Scripture.

To start off, God has desires, and all his desires are most certainly good. God declares, "I desire steadfast love and not sacrifice, the knowledge of God rather than burnt offerings" (Hosea 6:6). God also "desires all people to be saved and to come to the knowledge of the truth" (1 Timothy 2:4). As Jesus intercedes for future believers, he says, "Father, I desire that they also, whom you have given me, may be with me where I am" (John 17:24). God's desires are always good, but what about human desires?

It's no surprise that redeemed men and women created in the image of God can have correctly ordered desires as well. The psalmist writes, "Whom have I in heaven but you? And there is nothing on earth that I desire besides you" (Psalm 73:25). In Philippians 1:23, Paul says, "My desire is to depart and be with Christ, for that is far better." Paul also speaks of his "heart's desire and prayer to God" for the salvation of his fellow Jews (Romans 10:1). Augustine says this about good desires: "The whole life of a good Christian is an holy desire."[5]

But more often in Scripture, the concept of desire is presented negatively, not positively. In Genesis 3:6, desire is a key aspect of the Fall: "When the woman saw that the tree was good for food, and that it was a delight to the eyes, and that the tree was to be desired to make one wise, she took of its fruit and ate."

In Exodus 20:17, God delivers the last of the Ten Commandments: "You shall not covet your neighbor's house; you shall not covet your neighbor's wife, or his male servant, or his female servant, or his ox, or his donkey, or anything that is your neighbor's."

The Hebrew word *chamad*, rendered in this verse as "covet," can also be translated as "desire." Similarly in the Greek New Testament, the words *epithymeo* and *epithymia* can be rendered as "covet" or "lust" as well as "desire." In biblical terminology, lust and desire are not distinct categories. Desire doesn't *turn* into lust as many incorrectly assume, but wrongly ordered desire *is* lust.

How then do we differentiate between right and wrong desires?

The End of Desire

The moral value of any desire is determined by whether its "end" transgresses or conforms to God's standard. In fact, all desire is *teleological*.[6] The Greek word *telos* means "end, goal, or purpose." Thus, every desire has an end, goal, or purpose. Without an end, a desire simply wouldn't be desire.

Not only is every desire about *something*—tangible or intangible, but also every desire has an envisioned *purpose* or *action*. Old Testament scholar Brevard Childs explains that in Hebrew, desire is "an emotion which often leads to a commensurate action."[7] For us to evaluate desire, we must discern its end, purpose, or goal.

In Genesis 3, Adam and Eve desired to eat the fruit from the tree of the knowledge of good and evil—an action clearly forbidden by God. What made their desire wrong was not the *object*—the fruit, which in itself was good—but the *intended action* of their desire. If the end is sinful, then the desire is sinful as well.

In the Sermon on the Mount, Jesus teaches if the intended action is sinful, then the desire is sinful too. "You have heard that it was said, 'You shall not commit adultery.' But I say to you that everyone who looks at a woman with lustful intent has already committed adultery with her in his heart" (Matthew 5:27–28).

Jesus tethers the sinful sexual *act* of the seventh commandment ("You shall not commit adultery") to the sinful sexual *desire* of the tenth commandment ("You shall not covet your neighbor's wife").[8] In other words, it's wrong to say that only the *act* of illicit sex is sin; its *desire* is sinful as well.

Obviously, adultery and lust aren't exactly the same, just as murder and hate aren't the same. But the Son of God is making a provocative point: actual sin isn't birthed in innocence. Jesus condemns the desire to sin—which many mistakenly view as harmless—to be just as sinful as the egregious act. The only sexual revolution Jesus advocates is one that raises the bar on sexual purity and warns that sinful sexual desire is not something to toy with or treat trivially.

To be clear, sexual desire isn't bad in itself and can be good. It all depends on whether its *end* aligns with God's will. For example, in the wedding celebrated in the Song of Solomon, the bride exults, "I am my beloved's, and his desire is for me" (7:10). This mutual delight is both blessed and celebrated by God. However, the bride's desires before marriage needed to be restrained, as the bride herself affirms: "I adjure you, O daughters of Jerusalem . . . that you not stir up or awaken love until it pleases" (2:7; 3:5).

So what does all this tell us about the moral value of same-sex desire? Is it good or sinful?

The Most Common of Affections

First, we need to delineate different types of same-sex desire. How? By looking at its end. The end of same-sex *sexual* desire is sexual intimacy between two men or two women—which is sinful behavior. If the end is wrong, then the desire is wrong. Thus, same-sex sexual desire *per se* is sinful.

However, not all same-sex desire is sexual or erotic. There's also non-erotic same-sex desire. It's obvious that longings to form deep, nonerotic, *platonic* bonds of friendship with other members of the same sex are certainly blessed by God. Yet we shouldn't equate such platonic desires with sexually related desires. The God-given reality is that everyone desires healthy, nonsexual, same-sex friendships.

If a purely platonic desire for friendship, intimacy, companionship, and community were a part of one's "sexual orientation," then *everyone* would be "gay." Conflating platonic desires with sexual desires blurs the boundaries and ultimately makes the concept of same-sex attraction meaningless. Even gay neuroscientist Simon LeVay considers platonic desires for friendship to be an unreliable criterion for sexual orientation.[9]

If sexuality includes platonic desires, then this implies that same-sex-attracted individuals are inherently *better* at making same-sex friends than those with opposite-sex attractions. This is altogether not true. Simply put, platonic desires for friendship are not exclusive to or even stronger in those with same-sex attractions. These are affections common to everyone.

Awakening Romance

Another familiar mistake is the failure to recognize that some same-sex desires, although nonsexual, are nevertheless *romantic,* not platonic.

Romantic desires and platonic desires are not equivalent. It's crucial to distinguish between them because the end of romantic same-sex desire is not God's will.

Merriam-Webster defines *platonic* as "a relationship marked by the absence of romance or sex."[10] The *Oxford English Dictionary* defines *romance* as "ardour or warmth of feeling in a love affair; love, esp. of an idealized or sentimental kind."[11] Nonsexual romantic desires are essentially yearning to become *one* with and be permanently and exclusively united to someone we hold dear.

While lacking eroticism, when these romantic affections are toward a person in which a biblical covenantal union cannot occur, they are still wrong. Romance and love aren't synonymous. While friendship, kinship, and marriage are all contexts in which to experience love, there isn't one better or worse, greater or less than the other. Yet, Scripture only refers to marriage as becoming one—friendship isn't meant to replace marriage.

Some argue that it's an unbearable burden for same-sex-attracted individuals to constantly have to parse out which nonsexual desires are platonic (permissible) and which are romantic (not permissible). But spotting romantic desires isn't as hard as some make it. Romance is present when your heart races when you think about him. Throughout the day, you ponder, *Does she miss me right now?* Your thoughts are fixated on planning out details of what you'll do next with him. You're jealous when she shows more interest in another. You get lost in his eyes. Her touch sends chills up your spine. You want him completely to yourself. You cry for days when the relationship changes or ends.

Every single desire we have must be put to the test. What is its end, goal, or purpose? If you're biblically married and your romantic desires are for your spouse, those desires are good and blessed. If you're single and have romantic desires for someone of the opposite sex who is a potential spouse in biblical marriage, then those romantic desires are permissible.

All other romantic desires are improper and should not be allowed to grow or flourish. That's true for everyone—male or female, opposite-sex attracted or same-sex attracted.

Many end up in much pain when they naively allow their hearts to open to romantic desires when no God-honoring end is in sight. Unfortunately, these desires can so easily push people toward sinful behavior and, ultimately, away from Christ. John Piper wisely notes that "Christianity is war. It is a declaration of all-out combat against our own sinful impulses."[12] This truth applies to every believer—especially the individual entertaining same-sex romance.

What might seem like a simple confusion or conflation of desires can lead to sin. Same-sex romantic desires are not innocuous or innocent. Many same-sex-attracted individuals have allowed their romantic "crushes" and desires for their friends of the same sex to swell and intensify unchecked. This unguarded carelessness has led to unhealthy codependency, relational idolatry, sinful fantasies, sexual immorality, intense emotional distress, one-sided heartbreaks, severe depression, and even suicidality.

This may seem like a lot of restrictions on desires—namely, that same-sex romantic and erotic desires should not be celebrated and thus should be curbed. Does this then mean a life of isolation and loneliness for the individual with same-sex attractions and a constant fear that a regular friendship can turn romantic? As Christians, while guarding against sinful sexual and romantic desires, we are called to strengthen and deepen the bonds of relational intimacy within the context of the family of God, the church.

The church is the true and eternal family in which real, lasting, and genuine relationships should blossom and grow. I will discuss this concept of spiritual family further in a following chapter. But let us flee desires that draw us away from God and wholeheartedly chase after Christ and his bride with a profound desire to deepen brotherly, sisterly, platonic intimacy within the family of God.

Still, some believe that same-sex romantic desires aren't sinful because opposite-sex romantic desires are permissible. But these two scenarios aren't analogous. For two unmarried people of the opposite sex, a romantic relationship with careful restraint can culminate in a union blessed by God. But a same-sex romantic relationship can never culminate in a union blessed by God.

A more fitting analogy would be a married man in a romantic relationship with a woman who is not his wife. Regardless of the fact that they're *not* having sex, their romance is sinful. And in line with Jesus's words in Matthew 5:27–28, if the end is wrong (action) and the lust is wrong (desire), then everything in between is wrong as well (including romance). Romantic same-sex desires are not to be toyed with but should be resisted and mortified.

Actually, *every* Christian—whether experiencing opposite-sex attractions or same-sex attractions—should continuously and carefully parse and evaluate personal desires. Vigilance is a sign of spiritual maturity. A sinful act never comes out of nowhere but is birthed in the crevices of our hearts and minds, the seedbed of our desires. We must diligently learn the intentions and limits of our desires to know which to embrace (such as platonic same-sex desires) and which to resist (romantic and erotic same-sex desires).

Sexual expression is judged by the benchmark of holiness, a standard that isn't based on the heterosexual versus homosexual paradigm. Likewise, holy sexuality—faithfulness in marriage and chastity in singleness—is the only correct end for desire.

"SEXUAL ORIENTATION"

Blind Acceptance or Critical Assessment?

One of the things lacking today is a robust theological discussion on sexual orientation. This broadly used term, which some believe describes not only *how* we are but also *who* we are, definitely requires more in-depth analysis and evaluation. Should we simply accept this as a reality, as the only terminology to describe enduring same-sex attractions? Or should we step back and critically assess this idea in light of God's grand story—creation, fall, redemption, and consummation?

The modern concept of sexual orientation originates from the discipline of psychology, and often Christian discussions are built more around this social scientific framework than around a biblical one. It's important to recognize that this notion is rooted in a secular understanding of anthropology, which rejects or at least diminishes the reality of original sin.[1] In today's world of infinite shades of gray, sloppy ambiguity on biblical sexuality is essentially flirting with heresy.

For example, the idea that same-sex sexual orientation is only a disability (that is, a natural consequence of the Fall, like deafness) and not a moral consequence is dangerously close to Pelagianism, a denial of original sin. A naturally occurring disease or disability has no *direct* correlation to sinful behavior, while same-sex sexual orientation does. Remember that the doctrine of original sin is a key aspect to understanding same-sex sexual expression, desires, and temptations.

Gay activists carelessly brush off the Bible with the assumption that God's Word has nothing to say about "sexual orientation."[2] After all, they assert, this term or concept doesn't appear anywhere in the pages of the Bible. This strict and narrow understanding would not allow us to develop any biblical ethic or theology for today. Just because a term or concept isn't found in Scripture doesn't mean the Bible has nothing to say about it.

Our solution begins by looking to Scripture with an eye on creation, fall, redemption, and consummation—just as we did with holy sexuality. Secular categories don't always fit into biblical ones. Often there isn't an exactly equivalent paradigm, which requires us to assess the category and consider recategorizing. If we're able to reframe around a biblical framework, this will often bring more clarity and dispel confusion.

To begin, we must define *sexual orientation*. Regrettably, this crucial first step is frequently disregarded, but constructive dialogue can't occur without it. Many talk about sexual orientation, but few can explain precisely what it is. The American Psychological Association provides this explanation:

> Sexual orientation refers to an enduring pattern of emotional, romantic, and/or sexual attractions to men, women, or both sexes. Sexual orientation also refers to a person's sense of identity based on those attractions, related behaviors, and membership in a community of others who share those attractions.[3]

It's nearly impossible to disassociate sexual orientation from personal identity. This definition from the American Psychological Association clearly links the two. In previous chapters, we've already exposed the problems of fusing sexuality with identity and the error of making desire who we are.

From the definition above, we also see that orientation has a sociological aspect. That is, identifying oneself as a "gay Christian" implies that one identifies as much with the gay community as with the Christian community, if not more. Should Christ's body be placed at the same level with any demographic? This is one reason I never identify as a Chinese Christian or even a male Christian.

The above definition also describes *orientation* as "an enduring pattern" of attractions. Although attractions are part of this definition, we must not confuse orientation with them. "Enduring" communicates that these desires are persistent and don't readily go away. The American Psychological Association has stated that these attractions are generally not chosen.[4] But what exactly does "pattern" mean? Let's look at other definitions for more clarity.

In 2006 several international human rights activists produced the Yogyakarta Principles that defined *sexual orientation* as a "capacity for profound emotional, affectional and sexual attraction."[5] In his book *Gay, Straight, and the Reason Why: The Science of Sexual Orientation,* Simon LeVay defines *sexual orientation* as "the trait that predisposes us to experience sexual attraction."[6]

Aside from the ontological (identity) and the sociological (community) aspects, sexual orientation seems to convey a capacity or predisposition for sexual desire that is enduring and unchosen. With this understanding, do any existing biblical categories speak into this concept?

A Biblical Orientation Paradigm

Instead of differentiating between opposite-sex desires and same-sex desires, let's use the biblical categories of good desires and sinful desires.

Good sexual desires are those whose end is biblical marriage. Sinful sexual desires are those whose end is outside the context of biblical marriage.

Is there an existing biblical concept to address a capacity or predisposition for enduring, unchosen sinful desires? I believe there is. It's called a sinful nature—in other words, a sinful orientation.

Some English translations of the New Testament render the Greek word *sarx* as "sinful nature," while others render it literally as "flesh." *Sarx* is an important and particular concept in Paul's theology. Pauline expert Douglas Moo explains that especially in Paul's writings (such as in Romans and Galatians) the meaning of *sarx* is "the limitations of the human condition that have been imposed by sin."[7]

In Galatians 5:16–17, Paul explains how the flesh fights against the Spirit and the Spirit fights against the flesh. This dichotomous tension doesn't suggest that we have split natures inside us warring against each other; rather, *sarx* refers to the *whole* person marked by the rebellion—the "corruptibility and mortality"—of this present evil age.[8]

This reflects the redemptive-historical reality between the old self, characterized by the flesh, and the new self, characterized by the Holy Spirit of God. This tension between flesh and Spirit is evidence of the overlap between the present evil age and the coming age. The flesh represents this wicked era and our position under the dominion of sin and death. The Spirit represents the coming age and our freedom from the power of sin and the law.[9] In this overlap, aspects of both ages are present together.

The reality is that "the present evil age" (Galatians 1:4) has not passed away and the implications of sin and the "old man" linger. As redeemed believers, though we're being renewed and transformed day by day, we live nonetheless with the vestiges of our old self and with our distorted post-Fall image. This is why we must be vigilant in the midst of temptations. Unlike Jesus, who had no sinful nature, we have a "landing pad" for those temptations that can quickly turn into sinful desire.[10]

A spiritual battle is raging "between God's Spirit and the impulse to sin."[11] This impulse no longer enslaves the believer, but it can still have an influence. We therefore face a daily fight. In Romans 8:13, Paul pleads with us: "If you live according to the flesh you will die, but if by the Spirit you put to death the deeds of the body, you will live."

Christ's salvific work certainly has inaugurated a new era, but this new era is also not fully consummated. This is what theologians call the "already but not yet." We've been set free, but we must continue with perseverance in the battle until that final and glorious day arrives. What does all this mean for those of us who have a predisposition for same-sex sexual and romantic desires? There are a couple of things to point out.

Living in the Already but Not Yet

For the Christian, a predisposition doesn't mean an inescapable predetermination. In Romans 6:6–7, Paul explains that the individual at the moment of regeneration is emancipated from the bondage of sin and fallen human nature: "We know that our old self was crucified with him in order that the body of sin might be brought to nothing, so that we would no longer be enslaved to sin. For one who has died has been set free from sin."

This freedom from sin's reign doesn't imply freedom from all sinning or a complete absence of temptations, but it's a decisive break with sin and a qualitative change in which our mind is less dark and our will is less rebellious. This new life is the sovereign work of God.

The Holy Spirit is the divine cause of our rebirth (John 3:5–6), and this freedom from sin is an act of God's grace: "Sin will have no dominion over you, since you are not under law but under grace" (Romans 6:14). As

John Piper explains, "Grace is not simply leniency when we have sinned. Grace is the enabling gift of God not to sin. Grace is power, not just pardon."[12]

The other thing to remember is our need to avoid extremes. At one extreme, we must not to cheapen God's grace and assume that we can keep on sinning because "love covers a multitude of sins" (1 Peter 4:8). This would be a distortion, and Paul speaks directly to this: "Are we to continue in sin that grace may abound? By no means! How can we who died to sin still live in it?" (Romans 6:1–2).

But at the other extreme, some who have same-sex sexual temptations are overburdened with shame and guilt because they feel they aren't worthy of God's grace. They have repented and are not acting out but believe this struggle is the unpardonable sin. By recognizing that the issue is our flesh—our fallen human nature—we can daily realize that we're actually not that much different from anybody else. At the root, it all comes down to original sin. Every person has been corrupted by the moral consequence of the Fall. The exact form of temptation may be different, but the root cause is still the same. The issue is not whether we're tempted but how we respond.

Comfort comes from knowing that we're not alone. We need to be honest and transparent with trusted others about our struggles with unchosen and often ongoing temptations. However, further segregating ourselves into straight Christians and gay Christians gives the false impression that we're fundamentally different at the core of our being. We need more unity, not less, and this segregation by "orientation" is in essence a form of affective apartheid.

Instead, let's find solidarity in the fact that we all suffer from original sin—the moral consequence of the Fall—and that we're all in need of grace. Together we remind one another of our desperate need for the only solution for our sin nature: Christ and his body, the church.

THE BIBLICAL COVENANT OF MARRIAGE

More Than Companionship

As a policy, I never travel alone, and I'm blessed my mother has committed to travel with me wherever I go as my prayer warrior and someone to hold me accountable when I'm on the road. One Friday in April 2008, my mom was traveling with me during what could have been a disastrous situation.

We were flying out of Chicago, headed to Louisiana. I was officiating at a wedding the next day for my good friends Ryan and Hannah. As we checked our bags, the ticket counter representative gave my mother a boarding pass but said I would get mine at the gate. Strange—but she reassured me I had a seat for the flight to Baton Rouge.

At the gate, I asked the agent about my boarding pass and was told to wait patiently until my name was called. We waited at the gate for about half an hour before they started to board the plane. When I asked again about my boarding pass, I was told again to wait. The agent politely told my mother to go ahead and board the plane.

Not long after my mother boarded, the agent closed the door of the jet bridge. I've been flying long enough to know that once the door of the jet bridge closes, they do *not* open it for more passengers. I rushed to the agent and told her I needed to get on that flight. She apologized and explained there was a weight restriction, so no one else could get on the plane. She calmly explained she could definitely rebook me for the next flight . . . tomorrow.

I panicked and explained that if I would've known what was happening, I would've switched with my mother, who could fly out the next day. But I *had* to get on that flight. I explained that I was marrying someone and if I didn't get on, I'd miss the wedding. To my surprise, the agent told me to wait and sprinted down the jet bridge. She returned out of breath and told me to follow her quickly, which I did.

On the plane, I told my mother to get up because we had to switch places. The agent quickly put her hand on my mother's shoulder to keep her in her seat, then looked at me and said, "There's no way I'm going to allow your mother to miss your wedding!"

My mother and I had a good laugh once we were up in the air, and it turned out to be a great story to tell as a part of my wedding sermon the next day. For one moment in my life, I experienced what it was like to be a groom—at least in one person's eyes!

This whole episode caused me to wonder. If the truth was known about my relationship status and there was no wedding in Louisiana, would I have received such an extraordinary break-the-rules kind of reaction from the agent? Did this woman's reflex decision to move heaven and earth for me and my mother—which I greatly appreciated—reflect how much sentimentality we place on weddings and marriage and how little we place on singleness?

Jim Elliot, martyred missionary to the Auca Indians, had an aversion to the pomp and extravagance of weddings. As a young single man, he wrote, "Twentieth-century Christian weddings are the vainest, most meaningless forms" and "There is something in me that resists the showy part of weddings."[1] True to form, Jim and his wife, Elisabeth, were wed "without a fuss" in a simple ten-minute civil union ceremony in Quito, Ecuador, with four friends in attendance.

While I don't share the same disdain for weddings as Jim Elliot, I do question the profligacy inherent in many of them. Is it all truly necessary and God honoring? Did God really intend weddings to be *only* about the bride on her "special day" while essentially putting God on the back burner? Tens of thousands of dollars and countless weeks and months of planning are not unusual.

Without question, marriage is one of the most important covenants two people can make, and no one should take it lightly. But sentimentalizing marriage is not what God intended. Overromanticizing this holy union puts us at risk of idolizing it.

There's such a stark contrast between general responses to marriage and those to singleness. When we find out a friend just met someone, we exclaim, "I'm so happy for you! Is this *the one*?" When a single person suggests to her pastor that she may be called to singleness, the pastor's response is grave concern: "You'd better pray and fast about this. Singleness is not easy." I wonder—maybe we should switch our responses. This may result in fewer "Christian" marriages ending in divorce.

In the previous chapters, we've discussed identity, the image of God, sin, sex, temptations, desire, and sin nature. Now we must further flesh out the concept of holy sexuality: faithfulness in marriage and chastity in singleness. Many evangelicals are passionate about defending the sanctity of marriage, yet few can articulate a robust theology of marriage.

The next two chapters will provide a biblical and theological vision for marriage, and the two chapters following will express a biblical and theological vision for singleness.

Marriage as an Idol

From 1987 to 1997, *Married with Children* aired on television. It was a popular show about the Bundy family. Al, his wife, Peggy, and their two children were rude and crude—the antithesis of the polite and polished sitcom families of the 1980s and 1990s. This ragtag group of four represented everything family and marriage should *not* be. Actually, if we're clear about what marriage should *not* be, we're in a better position to know what it *should* be.

Without question, marriage is a major theme in the Bible. Almost every book of the Bible mentions it, with good examples and bad ones. God's story line begins with Adam and Eve and goes on to include Abraham and Sarah, Isaac and Rebekah, and on and on. Marriage is shown as the most physically and emotionally intimate of all human relationships on this side of glory. It's a coming-together union of two people, male and female. It is, without question, a good thing.

Some biblical examples of marriage are metaphorical. In the Old Testament, Yahweh was the faithful husband who made a covenant with his bride, Israel. He continued being faithful to her even when she was unfaithful to him, like an adulteress turning to other gods (Isaiah 54:5; Jeremiah 3:20; 31:32; Ezekiel 16:8; Hosea 2:16, 19–20). In the New Testament, Jesus is the bridegroom preparing his bride, the church, for the glorious wedding supper of the Lamb (Ephesians 5:25, 32; Revelation 19:7).

Scripture gives a unified canonical witness to the goodness of the marital union between husband and wife. Marriage—as defined by the Bible—is good. Yet in our passion to defend the goodness of biblical marriage, we may have turned marriage into an idol. I can hear some of you protesting, "What? How can marriage be an idol?" Let me explain. The most deceptive form of idolatry is when we worship something good. Good things aren't meant to be worshipped.

Idolatry occurs when we worship the gift, not the Giver; the blessing, not the One who blesses. Tim Keller defines an idol as "anything more important to you than God, anything that absorbs your heart and imagination more than God, anything you seek to give you what only God can give."[2]

Do you seek marriage to give you what only God can give? Has marriage become more important than God? Have we made marriage an end in itself? In *Marriage: Sex in the Service of God,* British scholar Christopher Ash explains, "When the relationship of the couple is considered as an end in itself it becomes an idol."[3]

In many ways, America's penchant for idolizing marriage brought about the watershed moment on June 26, 2015. In a highly contentious 5–4 decision (*Obergefell v. Hodges*), the US Supreme Court made same-sex marriage legal in all fifty states. Not only did it redefine marriage, but it also legally ratified the falsity that marriage is the pinnacle of love. The last paragraph of the majority opinion by Justice Kennedy reads, "No union is more profound than marriage, for it embodies the highest ideals of love, fidelity, devotion, sacrifice, and family."[4]

I respectfully but resolutely disagree.

Marriage may be an expression of love, but it's not the highest ideal of love. *God* is. As a matter of fact, Scripture tells us that "God is love" (1 John 4:8). In the entirety of recorded human history, no other religion or holy book has ever claimed this about its god. Only the Bible explicitly, coherently, and audaciously claims that the God it tells about *is* love. Other religions can claim that their god or gods may be loving. However, love is an ontological reality of our God. Understanding this point is fundamental when distinguishing Christianity from other religions and worldviews.

Let me further elucidate how Justice Kennedy's assertions are found lacking when measured against biblical truth. Marriage may be an expression of *fidelity,* but it's not the highest ideal of fidelity. *God* is. No one is more faithful than God. Marriage may be an expression of *devotion,* but no one is more devoted than God himself. Marriage may be an expression of *sacrifice,* but no sacrifice is greater than the One who gave his life for us! Marriage may be where *family* begins, but the only true and lasting family is the family of God, the body of Christ.

Marriage has never had a monopoly on love. The greatest expression of love is when God the Father sent his only begotten Son to die for us. The pinnacle of love is God's love for us in Christ. Nothing is greater than that!

Should marriage bring us joy and contentment? Certainly! But our ultimate joy and contentment must be in God alone—whether we're married or whether we're single. David exclaims to God, "Your steadfast love is better than life" (Psalm 63:3). Our ultimate goal in life is not marriage but Jesus Christ. And loving him more than life itself is the best way to prepare for marriage—or any other relationship. Christ did not die so we could be married. Christ died so we would have him.

Not the Cure for Loneliness

Justice Kennedy summarizes the rallying cry for same-sex couples: "Their hope is not to be condemned to live in loneliness, excluded from one of civilization's oldest institutions."[5] This view is held not only by Supreme Court justices but also by many others. So this raises the question, Is marriage *the* cure for loneliness? Many Christians would say yes and even quote Scripture to back up this misunderstanding.

In the second chapter of Genesis—following God's repeated declarations that his creation was "good"—comes a jarring pronouncement that something was *not* good: "It is not good that the man should be alone" (verse 18). The stark contrast between "good" in Genesis 1 and "not good" in Genesis 2 is not what we'd expect in God's perfect garden. Evidently, something else was necessary for the man's situation to become good.

We must note that Adam never made mention of being alone, nor did he complain about being lonely. God didn't consult our ancient progenitor about his feelings before making this divine assessment. The Creator observed, evaluated, and then rectified by creating woman.[6] With Eve at his side, Adam was no longer alone, and his situation was no longer "not good."

We must then consider this question: What precisely was not good? Christopher Ash explains the importance of this question: "If we can discern what was 'not good' . . . we shall understand theologically the true 'good' of marriage."[7]

"The reason for marriage," writes author and counselor Jay E. Adams, "is *to solve the problem of loneliness. . . . Companionship,* therefore, is the essence of marriage."[8] Christian counselor M. Blaine Smith writes, "Only one reason is mentioned for God's bringing Eve into Adam's life—the fact that Adam needed companionship. . . . God deems that others will be led by their own companionship needs to seek a spouse."[9]

Companionship, no doubt, is an important aspect of the marital union. For example, many widows experience intense grief after the death of their beloved spouse. Like our triune God, we're relational beings, and spouses provide companionship. Without question, marriage is one way God provides to meet that need.

However, we must be careful not to reduce marriage to merely companionship. If the sole function of marriage is to fulfill our human need for companionship, this elevates individual needs above everything else. In the life of a sinner, this can breed egocentrism, narcissism, and self-centeredness—personal traits that should never be the foundation of any marriage.

Although marital intimacy "may be one of the ways in which God remedies human loneliness, the Bible does not teach that it is the only, or even the major, remedy."[10] Companionship cannot be *the* essence of marriage. This would elevate marriage as some type of magical antidote for loneliness, yet we all probably know someone married who's still miserably lonely!

If marriage were necessary for companionship, then singleness would imply a lack of it; the inability to marry would mean a life doomed to loneliness. This warped view has led a growing number of "progressive" Christians to embrace same-sex marriage. Their reasoning usually goes like this: imposing singleness and not allowing someone to marry is cruel and unfair.[11] Paul Avis, an Anglican ecumenist, believes same-sex marriage is "the lesser of two evils, the greater evil being enforced celibacy and the accompanying loneliness."[12]

Many Christians buy into this bad logic that since Genesis 2:18 states that being alone is "not good," then singleness must be bad. Jay E. Adams has written that "God's fundamental evaluation of the single life is that it is 'not good.'"[13] I wonder whether the apostle Paul agrees with that verdict. Are children and teenagers who are too young to marry "not good"? And let's not forget that our Lord Jesus Christ while on earth was also single. Dare we say it was "not good" for him to be single?

Conflating singleness with loneliness, as you see, inevitably leads to a distorted Christology. The view that singleness is bad and marriage is better or best stems from the faulty conclusion that the only ideal form of companionship is marriage—thus, no marriage must somehow mean loneliness.

We must affirm that singleness is not equivalent to loneliness. Nor is being alone equivalent to being lonely. As an extrovert, I've learned to treasure my times of solitude. Some introverts plan vacations by themselves with a good book. Being alone doesn't necessarily mean loneliness. On the flip side, even married people wrestle with loneliness.

We all desire companionship. This desire isn't ultimately fulfilled in marriage or even intimate friendships. A single friend struggling with loneliness shouldn't be pushed toward the false ideal of marriage as the panacea. We should first point him to deeper intimacy with God, to the sufficiency of Christ, and to the fellowship of the church.[14] No spouse or friend should ever have the sole burden of meeting all our needs.

True Help

In Genesis 2:18, God said it was "not good" that Adam was alone. God didn't intend for us to be alone, and we're all created to desire companionship. But it's important to realize that God didn't simply provide Adam a companion or best friend; God provided a wife. I explained above that companionship is not the only aspect of marriage. God blessed Adam with Eve as a companion but, more importantly, as his "helper." By understanding the meaning of "helper," we'll better discern the true good of marriage.

Let's reread Genesis 2:18, paying particular attention to the second half of the verse: "It is not good that the man should be alone; I will make him a helper fit for him." The Hebrew word *'ezer* means "help" or "assistance" and occurs twenty-one times in the Old Testament.[15] Sixteen of these occurrences refer to God as Israel's help.

In Exodus 18:4, Moses named his son Eliezer (literally, "my God is help") and said, "The God of my father was my help, and delivered me from the sword of Pharaoh." God wasn't simply a companion to Moses— God delivered Moses. In Psalm 115:9, the writer declares, "O Israel, trust in the LORD! He is their help and their shield." Yahweh's help wasn't simply companionship—God protected Israel.

Psalm 121 begins, "I lift up my eyes to the hills. From where does my help come? My help comes from the LORD, who made heaven and earth." As the psalm continues, we see that "help" means that God protects us, never sleeps, provides shade, and keeps us from evil (verses 1–8).

Far from possessing the rather passive nature of simply being a companion, "help" conveys the concept of a person who acts and assists in fulfilling a task. Eve is thus the remedy for Adam's aloneness by being a companion *and* by assisting him in completing a mission. Christopher Ash aptly explains, "When we are told that Adam needs a 'helper,' [it] is connected with the work he has been given to do. He needs someone to come to his aid, for he cannot do this work 'alone.' "[16]

What was Adam's task? Let's look at two earlier verses: Genesis 2:15 and 1:28. Genesis 2:15 provides the intent for Adam's placement in Eden: "The LORD God took the man and put him in the garden of Eden to work it and keep it." Those Hebrew verbs as adverbial infinitives, *work* and *keep*, communicate purpose.[17] In other words, Adam's God-given *purpose* was to work and keep the garden.

These verbs *work* and *keep* occur together in thirteen other Old Testament verses, and all but two refer to some form of worship.[18] New Testament theologian Greg Beale is an expert on the eschatological significance of temple theology throughout the Old and New Testaments. He shows several parallels between the temple and the Garden of Eden, with the garden-sanctuary as a prototype of the tabernacle, which foreshadowed the temple.[19] Thus, working and keeping were in essence priestly duties of worship in God's garden-sanctuary.

This help extended beyond the garden-sanctuary to the whole earth. In Genesis 1:28, God blesses Adam and Eve with this mandate: "Be fruitful and multiply and fill the earth and subdue it, and have dominion over the fish of the sea and over the birds of the heavens and over every living thing that moves on the earth."

These five verbs, *be fruitful, multiply, fill, subdue,* and *have dominio*, essentially make up the two royal duties of multiplying and ruling. They also coincide with the dual priestly duties, working and keeping, from Genesis 2:15.[20]

Without Eve, Adam wouldn't have been able to reproduce (be fruit-ful and multiply). Without Eve, Adam wouldn't have been able to rule (fill, subdue, and have dominion). Without Eve, Adam wouldn't have been able to work and keep. And this was "not good."

Christopher Ash's conclusion hits the bull's-eye: "Our need is not to turn from marriage to work, but rather to remember that marriage is in-stituted by the Creator in the context of meaningful work."[21] If marriage were only for companionship, marriage would be me-centered. Rather, marriage is God-centered. God brought Adam and Even together—and brings husband and wife together—to provide companionship and to enable them to fulfill the work of worshipping, serving, and obeying God.

Same Kind of Different

When his son announced that he was gay, Western Theological Seminary professor James Brownson wrote that he was forced to "reimagine" Scrip-ture and to look more deeply at the Bible "with fresh eyes" in light of his son's sexuality.[22] Not surprisingly, this precipitated his abandonment of biblical sexuality, and he no longer affirms that same-sex relationships are sinful.

One of the points he makes is in relation to the meaning of *helper* in Genesis 2:18: "I will make him a helper fit for him." Brownson believes that "fit for him" has nothing to do with the differences of sexes but has everything to do with similarity.[23] In other words, he believes this is about Adam and Eve being more similar to each other than to the rest of creation and not about their physiological differences as male and female. Thus, according to Brownson, sexual differentiation is not essential to marriage.

But this is far from what the text is communicating and fails to take into account the full breadth of what "fit for him" means. The Hebrew construction *kenegdo* has been translated "fit for him" and can have the sense of "like his opposite," communicating both similarity and dissimilarity.

Conveniently, Brownson dismisses this "notion of difference" simply because "difference remains undeveloped in the remainder of the passage."[24] But only selectively looking forward to "the remainder of the passage" while ignoring the previous context is hermeneutical tunnel vision and a textbook example of eisegesis—when an interpreter forces his own bias and ideas into the text.

In Genesis 1, the recurring theme of separating and binding is unmistakable: light and darkness, day and night, evening and morning, the waters and the heavens, land and sea, plants yielding seed and trees bearing fruit, sun and moon, birds and fish, livestock and beasts, and male and female.[25]

In Genesis 2, the garden-sanctuary repeats this theme of separating and binding via the "essential bonds between human and ground, human and animal, man and woman, and the human pair with God (2:4–24)."[26] It's difficult to get away from these two related concepts of *separating* and *binding* when reading Genesis 2:18.

Jesus confirms this integral creation theme of separating and binding. In Matthew 19:4–6 (and its parallel in Mark 10:6–9), the Son of God quotes briefly from Genesis 1:27 and 2:24. In doing so, he juxtaposes and conjoins the differentiation of the sexes in Genesis 1 (God "made them male and female," Matthew 19:4) with the union of the sexes in Genesis 2 ("the two shall become one flesh," Matthew 19:5).

Therefore, "fit for him" in Genesis 2:18 means *both* similarity and dissimilarity, not simply one or the other. The Hebrew construction *kenegdo* suggests "both likeness and difference or complementarity."[27] Dennis Hollinger, president of Gordon-Conwell Theological Seminary, explains, "It's a union between two who are alike as fellow-humans, and yet unalike as male and female."[28]

If Genesis 2, according to Brownson, is only about similarity, the Bible should elevate same-sex relationships as *better* than opposite-sex relationships because they're *more* similar. And if marriage is only about sameness, then shouldn't the Bible also elevate incestuous relationships, because what's more similar than blood sister, brother, mother, father, daughter, or son? The answer is obvious—*no!*

The Bible upholds sexual purity as a tension between similarity and complementarity—similar but not too similar, different but not too different. This comes out clearly in certain prohibitions in Leviticus 18: incest is too *similar,* thus sinful; same-sex relationships are too *similar,* thus sinful; bestiality is too *different,* thus sinful.

God intends sex to be enjoyed in marriage between a husband and a wife, with sexual complementarity as a core aspect. This makes husband and wife more similar than animals but more different than relatives and those of the same sex.

We've clarified what marriage is *not.* But what is marriage and its purpose? And how does God's grand story of redemption shape our understanding of this union between husband and wife?

A THEOLOGY OF MARRIAGE

The Meaning Behind "I Do"

A group of children were asked, "What is love?" Here are just a few of their answers:

> Love is when you kiss all the time. Then when you get tired of kissing, you still want to be together and you talk more. My Mommy and Daddy are like that. They look gross when they kiss.

> Love is when Mommy sees Daddy smelly and sweaty and still says he is handsomer than Robert Redford.

> Love is when Mommy gives Daddy the best piece of chicken.

> When my grandmother got arthritis, she couldn't bend over and paint her toenails anymore. So, my grandfather does it for her all the time, even when his hands got arthritis too. That's love.[1]

What is love? It's a question many adults have trouble answering. But notice how the answers from these children are all observations of their parents or grandparents. If you're married and a parent, do your children see love exemplified in your marriage?

I'd like to pose a question to those of us who defend the sanctity of marriage: What exactly is marriage? If we believe marriage is holy—which it is—we should be able to clearly articulate its purpose and meaning.

Marriage Is Covenant

The concept of covenant is implicitly conveyed in this foundational text for marriage:

Then the man said,

> "This at last is bone of my bones
>   and flesh of my flesh;
> she shall be called Woman,
>   because she was taken out of Man."

Therefore a man shall leave his father and his mother and hold fast to his wife, and they shall become one flesh. (Genesis 2:23–24)

Giving someone a name had profound meaning in the ancient Near Eastern world. God named Abraham and Israel when he entered into a covenant with each of them (Genesis 17:5; 35:10). In similar manner, in Eden, the man named the woman when he entered into the covenant of marriage with her.[2]

Old Testament scholar Walter Brueggemann believes that bone and flesh could also have a metaphorical meaning of strength and weakness, together constituting a covenantal formula.[3] In other words, Adam was committing to this covenant in times of strength as well as times of weakness. He was communicating that his covenant to Eve was unaffected by changing circumstances. "Bone of my bones and flesh of my flesh" implies a formula of constancy and abiding loyalty.[4]

Marriage Is One

"And they shall become one flesh" (Genesis 2:24). This "one flesh" concept is, by far, the most profound and fundamental statement on marriage in Scripture. Not only is this Edenic ideal a blueprint for the marriage covenant and a metaphor for the physical union of husband and wife, but it is also a divine covenantal pattern of the relationship between God and Israel permeating the Old and New Testaments. "One flesh" is the substructure for many key biblical texts discussing and defending marriage.

This phrase *one flesh* primarily denotes sex in marriage, but it also communicates something more profound than simply lovemaking: the marital covenant is a permanent, exclusive, and holistic union of two people. Dennis Hollinger explains that *one flesh* "points to the unique physical, emotional, and spiritual bond that occurs through sexual intercourse."[5]

The Hebrew word for "one" in this passage is *'echad*. We see the word again in Deuteronomy 6:4: "Hear, O Israel: The Lord our God, the Lord is one." Oneness in this verse is both unity and diversity—God is Father, Son, and Holy Spirit. Similarly, unity and diversity are expressed in the oneness of marriage as male and female.

The Hebrew word for "flesh" in Genesis 2 is *basar*, which refers not only to the soft tissue of a body but also to the entirety of a person.[6] Therefore, this one-flesh union in marriage is more than simply sex; it's an all-encompassing reality that fuses two diverse people into one.

In the New Testament, the Pharisees attempt to pull Jesus into the ongoing debate about whether divorce is allowable. In response to their disingenuous question, Jesus applies this paradigm of oneness, quoting from Genesis 2:24: "'Therefore a man shall leave his father and his mother and hold fast to his wife, and the two shall become one flesh.' So they are no longer two but one flesh" (Matthew 19:5–6; Mark 10:7–8). Nothing can be clearer than "one flesh" to communicate the indivisibility of marriage. It isn't just that marriage *should not* be separated; it *cannot.*[7]

Yet in light of this oneness, we must be careful to avoid a common misunderstanding. Husbands often joke that their wife is their *better half.* But according to Scripture, marriage is not two halves becoming one—it is two *wholes* becoming one. It's inaccurate for engaged individuals to say their fiancé completes them. No other person completes us. We're complete only in Christ. I often tell my students, "Be whole before you become one." When two incomplete people try to become one, they never become *one.* Instead, the result is a codependent mess.

If marriage is two becoming one, what about polygamy? Same-sex marriage advocates often purport that polygamy is one form of marriage in the Bible. However, when we study them closely, we see that the Bible uses those instances of polygamy to articulate a theology of disapproval.

Old Testament scholar Richard Davidson explains that the biblical examples of polygamy bristle with "discord, rivalry, heartache, even rebellion, revealing the negative motivations and/or disastrous consequences that invariably accompanied such departures from God's Edenic standard."[8]

Let's look at the first instance of polygamy found in Genesis 4:19: "And Lamech took two wives." What follows in Genesis 4:23–24 provides a glimpse into Lamech's heart—he's a violent and vengeful killer. "Lamech said to his wives: 'Adah and Zillah, hear my voice; you wives of Lamech, listen to what I say: I have killed a man for wounding me, a young man for striking me. If Cain's revenge is sevenfold, then Lamech's is seventy-sevenfold.'" Scripture's first reference of polygamy involves an ungodly and reprobate man. This theology of disapproval continues throughout the Old Testament.

For example, in Abraham's tents, take the strife between Sarai and Hagar; in Jacob's household, take the discord between Rachel and Leah. The witness against polygamy in the Old Testament is uniform, and a theology of disapproval is expressed in the text as a distortion of God's creation ordinance for marriage.

The New Testament is even clearer, as Jesus and Paul both affirm the "one flesh" paradigm of marriage (Matthew 19:5–6; Mark 10:8; 1 Corinthians 6:16; Ephesians 5:31). Jesus's response to why divorce was allowed may also be how he would've responded to why polygamy was allowed: "Because of your hardness of heart" (Matthew 19:8).[9]

John Chrysostom, the early church father whose name literally means "golden-mouthed," defends monogamous marriage by faithfully looking back to Genesis 1 and 2. He declared that if multiple wives had been God's intention for a man, then "when he had made one man, he would have formed many women."[10]

From the Beginning

In Mark 10:2–9, the Pharisees question Jesus about divorce. The Son of God's response is a forceful rebuke denouncing the practice of dissolving marriage for almost any reason and shining a light on the hardness of their hearts (verse 5). As we saw earlier, Jesus grounds his teaching on marriage in the creation narrative:

> From the beginning of creation, "God made them male and
> female." "Therefore a man shall leave his father and mother and
> hold fast to his wife, and the two shall become one flesh." So they

are no longer two but one flesh. What therefore God has joined together, let not man separate. (verses 6–9)

Jesus could have quoted from numerous passages to affirm the enduring nature of the marriage covenant, but nothing is more foundational than this Edenic prototype: the covenantal union between Adam and Eve.

God is Lord over marriage because he's the one who joins man and woman together. "Let not man separate" serves as our reminder that divorce runs contrary to God's creation ordinances "from the beginning." Men and women should not undo what God has done. Intentionally breaking up a marriage is in fact an attempt to usurp God. This was Jesus's way of displaying the antithesis between God who joins together and the first-century Jewish men who encouraged separation for essentially any reason.[11]

However, if all Jesus wanted to reaffirm was the indivisibility of marriage, the "one flesh" imagery from Genesis 2:24 would've been sufficient. But Jesus introduces the biblical concept of sexual differentiation from Genesis 1:27, which on the surface doesn't seem directly relevant: "God made them male and female" (Mark 10:6).[12] Yet for Jesus, it's immensely relevant: there's no marriage apart from the biblical paradigm of male and female. Jesus tethers the creation of "male and female" (Genesis 1:27) to the creation of "one flesh" marriage (Genesis 2:24). This beautifully illustrates that God both differentiates male and female at creation and unites male and female in marriage. Jesus is affirming that when God made male and female, our Creator already had in mind the marital union that followed.

David Gushee, who proclaims himself "America's leading evangelical ethics scholar," switched his position on same-sex marriage and now calls for "full acceptance of LGBT Christians." He believes that Jesus in

Mark 10 is addressing only divorce and that the passage is irrelevant to the discussion on same-sex marriage.[13]

However, because Jesus includes Genesis 1:27 in Mark 10:6—"God made them male and female"—Gushee's assertion doesn't hold up to scrutiny. On one hand, God differentiates the sexes in Genesis 1; on the other hand, he unites the sexes in Genesis 2. What Gushee misses is this: the Pharisees' question on divorce becomes subservient to Jesus's teaching on marriage. The Son of God teaches that marriage is both indissoluble and fundamentally male and female.

Another implication of connecting Genesis 1:27 with marriage must not be missed. Not only does this verse establish the reality of sexual differentiation, but more importantly, it's also the key verse from which the doctrine of the *imago Dei* emanates. In other words, Jesus proclaims in Mark 10:6–8 not only that male and female are essential to marriage but also that marriage points to the image of God—thus bringing together both the nature of marriage and the nature of humanity.

Therefore, marriage is not a basic human or civil right. As Christians, we have no rights; our only right is in Christ. Furthermore, sex is *not* about what adults are free to do with their bodies. "From the beginning," God created marriage to be an indissoluble covenant between "male and female" with a deep correlation to the image of God. Any distortion of marriage—whether divorce, adultery, premarital sex, or same-sex marriage—is not only contrary to God's will but also an affront to the very image of God.

Marriage's Goal

Both Paul and Jesus quote Genesis 2:24 as the foundational text for understanding marriage: "Therefore a man shall leave his father and mother and hold fast to his wife, and the two shall become one flesh" (Ephesians 5:31). The theology of marriage, as Jesus and Paul demonstrate, is built on this key aspect of "one flesh."

Significantly, Paul immediately adds, "This mystery is profound, and I am saying that it refers to Christ and the church" (verse 32). Paul further utilizes "one flesh" as his foundation to reveal the "profound" mystery and eschatological significance of marriage. Whereas Jesus teaches on the essence of marriage in Mark 10, Paul articulates the *end* or *purpose* of marriage in Ephesians 5.

The Greek word for "profound" in this verse is *mega*—literally, "great" or "important." Paul's reference to "mystery" is meant to communicate that the one-flesh union between husband and wife is a unique type of human relationship that points to something great and profound.

In the Old Testament, Yahweh—the Lord God—is the bridegroom of Israel.[14] The "profound" mystery Paul sees is how this typology is now reframed. Whereas in the Old Testament Yahweh is the bridegroom, in the New the bridegroom is Christ. Whereas in the Old Testament Israel is the bride, in the New the bride is the church.[15]

To be clear, Christ's relationship with the church is not *like* human marriage; rather, human marriage foreshadows the ultimate reality that is Christ and the church. The first marriage between Adam and Eve in Genesis 2:24 typologically corresponds to Christ and the church in the consummation.[16] Human marriage is only a prototype of the relationship between God and his people, with the ultimate eschatological archetype being Christ and the church.

Therefore, the purpose of human marriage isn't ultimately for the husband and wife to love each other. Marriage's true aim is to point people toward the ultimate and eternal reality of Christ and the church. Marriage is only a momentary shadow; Christ and the church are the perfect and everlasting reality.[17] But if Christ and the church are the reality, what happens to the shadow on the last day?

Jesus answers that in Matthew 22. The Sadducees, slyly questioning him about the seven-time widow of seven brothers, wonder whose wife she would be in the resurrection. Jesus's response must have astonished his hearers: "In the resurrection they neither marry nor are given in marriage, but are like angels in heaven" (Matthew 22:30; Mark 12:25; Luke 20:34–36).

The Sadducees didn't believe in the resurrection and supposed wrongly that if God did raise the dead, life in heaven would simply be an extension of life here on earth. They were gravely mistaken. In the resurrection, things won't be as they are now. Our physical bodies will be transformed (Philippians 3:21). There'll be a new heaven and a new earth (Revelation 21:1). There'll be no more tears, no more death, no more mourning, no more crying, and no more pain (Revelation 21:4).

Once this glorious truth is actualized in eternity, the earthly shadow of marriage is swallowed up by the perfect reality of Christ being wed to the church. There will be no more reason for the imperfect shadow of earthly marriage—yet, this doesn't mean all memories of earthly relationships will be erased.

It does mean that all believers will be wed to Christ and that our deepest affections and devotion will be toward Christ alone. Our time and energy will be spent in the fulfilling and awesome glory of worshipping and serving God in his presence. Nothing else will be important.

Although we won't be married in heaven, it will be better—guaranteed. Therefore, we shouldn't think about singleness as a temporary state before marriage. Rather, marriage is the temporary state before eternity.

Retired pastor Ken Smith recently became a widower. He'd been married to Floy for sixty years. It was through their love for the Lord and their love for the lost that my sister in Christ, Rosaria Butterfield, was gradually exposed to a holy and loving God.

After Floy's passing, many tried to comfort Pastor Ken. With good intentions some asked, "Don't you look forward to the day when you're reunited with your wife in heaven?" His response was always "I don't have a wife in heaven, but I'm certainly looking forward to being fully united to Christ." This is how he explained it to me in an email:

> When I was looking at my wedding ring and deciding whether or not to wear it, I pondered the marriage vows we had taken. The vows say "till death do us part" and "as long as we both shall live." Those thoughts led me to see our wedding as being "fulfilled." I mused on the idea of our marriage being fulfilled, and it gave me a new slant on thanksgiving for dear Floy. Our marriage was not interrupted but fulfilled! No need to talk about renewing our relationship as husband and wife in heaven. Our marriage was an "on earth" institution, and it is now fulfilled. So I took my ring off. Marriage completed. Interestingly enough, this brought me immense comfort, peace, and thanksgiving.

Good theology was Pastor Ken's comfort. His comment may seem odd for a man grieving the loss of his faithful and loving wife, but he was delineating the intensity of his grief as much as he was defending and celebrating Floy's complete union with her risen Savior—and the sure hope of his own future union and glorification.

Pastor Ken's wedding ring was a symbol of his earthly marriage to Floy. And now their marriage is "fulfilled" as she rests in the arms of our Lord. She, along with all the other saints who have gone before us—as Christ's bride-to-be—wait in eager anticipation for that wonderful day, the marriage supper of the Lamb (Revelation 19:6–9), when all the elect in consummated glory will together sing, "Let us rejoice and exult and give him the glory, for the marriage of the Lamb has come, and his Bride has made herself ready" (verse 7).

Marriage here on earth is not the ultimate; it's the penultimate. The ultimate awaits us in eternity, and you were created for it—regardless of whether you're single now or married. When you feel a certain discontent in your marriage, even when your marriage is healthy and good, *this is normal*. There's only one marriage that will bring you ultimate contentment. Heaven will mean complete union and consummated glory with Christ—what greater joy is there than that?

SINGLENESS

For Better or for Worse?

When I was three, my older brother was asked to be a ring bearer at a family friend's wedding. I was too young to remember, but apparently the flower girl threw a tantrum and refused to walk down the aisle. Being a cute, well-behaved boy, I was volunteered at the last minute to be my brother's sidekick.

A few years later, when I was eight, it was my turn to be a ring bearer, and the grandeur of the occasion fascinated me. Later that year, when the girls in my third-grade class performed a wedding ceremony on the playground, I acted as the bridegroom. The other boys teased me for participating, but even at that age, I knew I wanted to get married.

In China, parents place much emphasis on marriage. The pressure for adult singles to find a partner is so great that "renting" a girlfriend or boyfriend to bring home to appease pestering parents is a growing trend. Remaining single is even viewed as being rebellious rather than *xiào shùn* (showing filial piety).

In America, being unmarried is also cast in a negative light. From our childhood, we sense an undercurrent of negativity toward singleness. Take fairy tales, for example; how do they all end? They get married and live happily ever after. End of story. In actuality, the real lesson we should teach our children is this: ultimate contentment comes not from marriage but from an intimate relationship with Jesus Christ—whether we're married or whether we're single.

Jesus didn't die so we could get married; he died so we could have *him*. Dennis Hollinger says it best: "Life without sexual intimacy and marriage is not a deficient life. Rather, life without intimacy with God in Christ is deficient."[1] Human relationships are important and significant. However, "the chief end of man" is not to marry or to befriend others but "to glorify God, and enjoy him forever."[2]

I once knew a missionary who was unmarried when she left for the field. Like most Christian singles, she wanted to get married. After finishing her five-year term, she reconnected with old friends here in the US, and they chatted about her ministry overseas, future plans, and her personal life. They inevitably asked, "Are you dating anyone? Is there anyone special in your life?" Her simple and honest answer was "No, not yet." Their response caught her off guard. With deep concern and sometimes tears welling up in their eyes, they'd ask, "Can I pray for you?" It was almost as if she had cancer.

Is singleness a curse? A life sentence of misery? Christian singles don't need our pity. Singles need to be welcomed, valued, and loved as fellow sisters and brothers in Christ.

Although nearly half of American adults today are single, the percentage of singles who attend church is nowhere near this high.[3] We grieve that the rise in cohabitation and divorce among unbelievers, compounded by the fact that people are marrying later in life, contributes to this. Still, could our own churches be missing a significant demographic in our communities?

A well-known evangelical pastor was forthright in his opinion against the unmarried: "Biblically, singleness is not ideal."[4] Essentially, this pastor would rebuke all single men for being immature, selfish, and fearful of commitment. Certainly, some young singles are this way, but not all. Jesus and Paul were single, but they weren't immature, selfish, or fearful of commitment.

Our church bulletins are full of wonderful family-oriented programs, but they often lack anything for single adults. For many churches, the "college and career group" is really just an afterthought—a singles ghetto. A year will not go by without several much-needed sermons on marriage and family, but seldom do we hear entire sermons on the goodness of singleness.

Even our unspoken requirement for pastors to be married means that Jesus and Paul would be precluded from serving in the vast majority of evangelical churches today. This should concern us. In our vigorous defense of traditional marriage, have we misunderstood, undervalued, and distorted singleness?

You may be thinking, *What does a deficient view of singleness have to do with my gay loved one?* A lot. Since it's God's will for her or him to refrain from same-sex relationships, being single would be a part of their reality now and possibly much longer. Are our church communities a vibrant place for these singles to grow and thrive in their Christian faith?

Let's be honest: not really. Regrettably, this misunderstanding can be traced back in history.

Ancient Stigma

In Old Testament times, the Israelites held a less-than-positive picture of singleness. There's evidence in ancient Jewish tradition and rabbinic literature that Jewish men were under religious obligation to marry. In addition, Jewish husbands were obligated to have sexual relations with their wives to "be fruitful and multiply" (Genesis 1:28). Early marriage was strongly recommended.[5]

The accounts of singleness in the Old Testament are sparse. In fact, the Hebrew Bible has no word that strictly means "unmarried person."[6] The Old Testament concepts associated with an unmarried woman— *widow* and *virgin*—both assume that these persons would, at some point, be married.

Two Old Testament themes—*offspring* and one's *name*—had particularly significant implications for singles in ancient Israel. A lack of offspring and the inability to perpetuate one's name produced the greatest stigma for singles.

God commanded Jeremiah to forgo marriage and children (Jeremiah 16:2). This abstention was a visible symbol of his prophetic message—God's impending judgment on Judah.[7] Barry Danylak, who has written must-read books on a biblical theology of singleness, explains that "Jeremiah's lack of offspring was to model God's judgment on his people that they too would become bereft of their offspring."[8]

Throughout the Hebrew Bible, many offspring were seen as a blessing, and childlessness was regarded as a curse. "Behold, children are a heritage from the LORD, the fruit of the womb a reward. Like arrows in the hand of a warrior are the children of one's youth" (Psalm 127:3–4). From the first chapter in Genesis, there's an explicit association between reproduction and blessing: "And God blessed them. And God said to them, 'Be fruitful and multiply'" (Genesis 1:28).

The inability of Rachel, Jacob's wife, to bear offspring generated much grief and turmoil (Genesis 29:31; 30:1). For Hannah, who eventually became the mother of the prophet Samuel, years of barrenness precipitated sorrow, shame, and ridicule (1 Samuel 1:2–8).

The widow Naomi, Ruth's mother-in-law, experienced the death of her sons, who had both died childless. Naomi confessed that God had "brought calamity" and had dealt with her "very bitterly" (Ruth 1:20–21). What made her singleness so unbearable was the scourge of no offspring.

In Psalm 109:13, King David curses his opponent by saying, "May his posterity be cut off; may his name be blotted out in the second generation!" The continuation of one's name was a blessing, and the extinguishing of offspring and name seemed to embody God's covenantal curses.[9] In a world full of couples and children, the unmarried individual living in ancient Israel had little to no hope for a bright future.

Yet—doesn't God heed the call of the downcast and the cry of the poor? "The needy shall not always be forgotten," David writes, "and the hope of the poor shall not perish forever" (Psalm 9:18). But where in the Old Testament can we find hope for the single, for the one with no offspring or name?

Better Than Offspring

During a bleak and difficult time in the history of the nation of Judah, Isaiah prophesied of a bright and hopeful future. He spoke of a suffering servant—fulfilled later in the person of Jesus the Messiah—who would bring salvation and joy to everyone, even those with no offspring or name.

Isaiah tells how this hope was extended specifically to the eunuch, a despised figure who embodied the reality of having no offspring and no possibility of continuing his name. In light of the coming Messiah, Isaiah records God's words of hope to eunuchs: "I will give in my house and within my walls a monument and a name better than sons and daughters; I will give them an everlasting name that shall not be cut off" (Isaiah 56:4–5). Their exclusion is turned into inclusion. But what reward or blessing can be "better than sons and daughters"?

In Isaiah 61:8–9, God says, "I will make an everlasting covenant with them. Their offspring shall be known among the nations, and their descendants in the midst of the peoples; all who see them shall acknowledge them, that they are an offspring the LORD has blessed." This new, eternal covenant means not only that they will *have* offspring but also that they *are* offspring blessed by God.[10]

This is a radical paradigm shift. For so long, it was believed that entrance into the covenant required being born a Hebrew and that, under this old covenant, having offspring was a blessing. However, under the new covenant established in Jesus's blood (1 Corinthians 11:25), entrance requires being born again (John 3:3), and being the Lord's offspring *is* the blessing.

This new covenant is inaugurated by the life, death, and resurrection of Jesus Christ, and this new birth means being "born of water and the Spirit" (John 3:5). Spiritual birth makes us spiritual offspring: "For all who are led by the Spirit of God are sons of God" (Romans 8:14). What is better than having sons and daughters? It's *being* God's sons and daughters!

In Matthew 28:19, Jesus commissions his disciples to "make disciples of all nations." Being a disciple means being a born-again child of God, and making disciples means being used by him to bring "many sons to glory" (Hebrews 2:10). All God's children should be begetting spiritual children—whether married or single.

The apostle Paul was single and had no physical offspring. He was, however, a spiritual father to many spiritual sons and daughters. Paul calls Onesimus "my child" (Philemon 10); he calls Timothy "my beloved and faithful child in the Lord" (1 Corinthians 4:17); he calls Titus "my true child in a common faith" (Titus 1:4).

This apostle to the Gentiles refers to the Galatian Christians as "my little children" (Galatians 4:19) and reminds the believers at Corinth, "I became your father in Christ Jesus through the gospel" (1 Corinthians 4:15). There's no question that Paul, as a single man, fulfilled the creation mandate to "be fruitful and multiply" (Genesis 1:28).

When we look in the Old Testament, the emphasis is on marriage, family, and physical offspring. When we read the New Testament, the emphasis is on the family of God with a shift from physical offspring to spiritual offspring. Here is the radical truth on family that Jesus inaugurates through the new covenant: the people of the old covenant grew by procreation, while the people of the new covenant grow by regeneration.[11]

This is important today for singles as we live under the new covenant, especially in light of a world that places preeminence on marriage. Our earthly families are temporarily bound by blood, but the family of God is eternally bound by the blood of the Lamb. This family of God is the church, the bride of Christ. If we're born again, then we're sons and daughters of God. If we're God's sons and daughters, then we're all brothers and sisters. We are family!

With the inauguration of the new covenant, Jesus dramatically redefines the family.[12] Early in his ministry, his mother and brothers summon him (Mark 3:31). His response, seen in the context of first-century Israel, is truly scandalous: "Who are my mother and my brothers? . . . Here are my mother and my brothers! For whoever does the will of God, he is my brother and sister and mother" (verses 33–35). In other words, the new spiritual family takes precedence over the natural family.

Peter tells Jesus, "We have left our homes and followed you" (Luke 18:28). Jesus responds, "Truly, I say to you, there is no one who has left house or wife or brothers or parents or children, for the sake of the kingdom of God, who will not receive many times more in this time, and in the age to come eternal life" (verses 29–30). Here again we're promised something "better than sons and daughters" (Isaiah 56:5)—the blessing of doing the will of God and being part of his new family, the church.

As we've seen, the New Testament portrays the status of being unmarried in a much more affirmative manner than the Old Testament.

Of the three major monotheistic religions today—Judaism, Christianity, and Islam—only Christianity can claim a theology that affirms singleness.[13]

The most prominent unmarried individuals in the New Testament are Jesus and Paul, whose words compose the New Testament's main teaching on singleness. Our next chapter will be a closer look at what they both say.

13

MORE ON SINGLENESS

Simply a Good Gift

We often miss how radically countercultural it was for Jesus, a thirty-year-old in first-century Israel, to remain single. According to Jewish traditions, the proper age to marry was eighteen; if a man was twenty and unmarried, he was considered accursed.[1] This was also true for recognized teachers like Jesus; rabbis were expected to marry, with only one known rabbi during those times who remained single—and he was criticized for it.[2]

Twice in the New Testament, Jesus touches on the topic of singleness, both times in response to questions not specifically related to singleness. In these two responses, Jesus's profound and insightful words are indispensable to a biblical understanding of singleness in light of God's grand story—particularly as it relates to our loved ones with same-sex attractions.

"Receiving" Singleness

In Matthew 19:3–9, Jesus rebukes the Pharisees as they try to debate the topics of divorce, marriage, and remarriage. Having the last word, Jesus declares in verse 9, "Whoever divorces his wife, except for sexual immorality, and marries another, commits adultery." Although his hearers held fairly conservative views on marriage and divorce, Jesus's strict stance on remarriage was unprecedented.[3]

Not surprisingly, his disciples react to their master's radical teaching with this comment: "If such is the case of a man with his wife, it is better not to marry" (verse 10). Their cynical implication is this: *Are you really saying it is better not to marry?* They're giving Jesus an opening to back down from his supposedly rigid view and offer something more moderate and practical, something that would make marriage more appealing.[4]

Jesus replies in words that to us seem peculiar and enigmatic:

> Not everyone can receive this saying, but only those to whom it
> is given. For there are eunuchs who have been so from birth, and
> there are eunuchs who have been made eunuchs by men, and
> there are eunuchs who have made themselves eunuchs for the sake
> of the kingdom of heaven. Let the one who is able to receive this
> receive it. (verses 11–12)

Instead of defending marriage, Jesus unexpectedly makes an astonishing statement that affirms singleness—a point we can better discern from a closer look.

Taken literally, the word *eunuch* has little to do with marriage—especially making oneself a eunuch! But the disciples knew Jesus to be a master of metaphor and would have known this was a figure of speech. Earlier in the same gospel, Jesus exhorts sinners to tear out an eye and cut off a hand or foot (Matthew 5:29–30; 18:8–9). Without exception, every use of self-mutilation in the Gospels is figurative—including in this passage.

The Greek word *eunouchos* had developed connotations broader than the literal meaning, "castrated male." It even signified an animal or a plant that was not bearing offspring or seed.[5] In this verse's context of whether to marry, the eunuch is a metaphor for an unmarried individual unable to bear offspring. Both a eunuch "from birth" and a human-made eunuch represent those who are single involuntarily, while a self-made eunuch represents those who voluntarily choose to set aside marriage and offspring "for the sake of the kingdom of heaven."[6]

With these meanings in mind, let's look again at how Jesus prefaces his statement about these eunuchs in Matthew 19:11: "Not everyone can receive this saying, but only those to whom it is given." The Greek word translated "receive" means literally "have room for"—thus, in 2 Corinthians 7:2, "make room in your hearts." Here it refers to making room in one's mind. In other words, not everyone can mentally grasp, understand, or accept this saying.[7]

And when Jesus talks about receiving or understanding "this saying," what is he referring to? It's the saying his disciples have just made in verse 10: "If such is the case of a man with his wife, it is better not to marry."[8] It helps to recognize that the Greek word translated as "better" can also mean "advantageous." Therefore, Jesus's statement in verse 11 could be paraphrased in this way: "Not everyone can *understand* this saying—that it's *advantageous* not to marry—but only those to whom *the understanding* is given."

Jesus is not affirming that singleness is *comparatively* better than marriage, as some might believe; rather, in light of the kingdom of heaven, singleness is *advantageous* just as marriage is advantageous. This was the reality: no first-century Jew needed to be convinced that marriage was advantageous. However, few were truly able to *understand* the biblical teaching about the advantages of singleness in light of the kingdom of heaven.

Jesus's words in verse 11 help us comprehend the conclusion in verse 12: "Let the one who is able to receive this receive it." Many mistake this as Jesus setting up a distinction between those who have the ability or gift to forgo marriage and those who do not. This is not the case. What's being received is not an ability or gift of continence but the "saying" that singleness is good. In other words, the only gift here is the gift of understanding.

Jesus's conclusion in verse 12 can be paraphrased in this way: "Let the one who is able to *understand* this *saying—it's advantageous not to marry—understand* it." This echoes a similar challenge about the kingdom of heaven in Matthew 13:9: "He who has ears, let him hear."[9]

In Matthew 13:10, his disciples ask Jesus why he spoke to the crowd in parables, and his response includes a reference to Isaiah 6:9: "You will indeed hear but never understand, and you will indeed see but never perceive" (Matthew 13:14). Essentially, not hearing was a sign of God's judgment.[10]

Those who don't hear are just part of the undiscerning crowd, while those who do hear are true disciples of Christ.[11] Our Lord is inviting all of us with ears to hear to "receive" and understand that *singleness is good.* Not everyone is called to voluntarily forgo marriage, but all are called to "receive," understand, and affirm that voluntary and involuntary singleness is good.

Keeping in view the whole passage (Matthew 19:3–12), we see that Jesus unabashedly affirms that both biblical marriage and biblical singleness are good.

Single in Eternity

In Luke 20, the Sadducees "who deny that there is a resurrection" (verse 27) try to set up Jesus with a bizarre tale. If you remember, we looked at its parallel passage (Matthew 22) in a previous chapter. The oldest of seven brothers marries a woman but then dies with no offspring. The widow is passed from the second brother all the way down to the youngest, as one by one they die without offspring. Finally the wife dies as well.

Attempting to confound Jesus, the Sadducees ask, "In the resurrection, therefore, whose wife will the woman be?" (Luke 20:33). By reducing this story to an absurd conclusion, they attempt to disprove the resurrection. Seven husbands sharing one wife makes the idea of a resurrection seem preposterous. Here is Jesus's response:

> The sons of this age marry and are given in marriage, but
> those who are considered worthy to attain to that age and to
> the resurrection from the dead neither marry nor are given in
> marriage, for they cannot die anymore, because they are equal
> to angels and are sons of God, being sons of the resurrection.
> (verses 34–36)

The Sadducees incorrectly assume that the resurrected life will be the same as life in this age. Jesus contrasts the sons of this age who "marry and are given in marriage" with the sons of the resurrection who "neither marry nor are given in marriage." The current age is simply not like the next. New Testament scholar Darrell Bock tells us that "marrying and getting married are not a part of that future existence."[12]

Although sexual differentiation as male or female will continue into eternity, marriage as we know it will end. If marriage ends, sexual intercourse will end as well—since sex blessed by God occurs only within marriage. And if sex ends, then sexual desires will also have an end—since unfulfilled longings are not a part of our consummated reality (Revelation 21:4).

However, this is not a return to an Edenic, pre-Fall sexuality but a fulfillment of God's original plan. Just as the consummation of marriage results in fulfillment, so too the consummation of sexual expression and desires results in fulfillment. Sexuality, as we currently know it, will end.

Let that truth sink in. Sex and marriage are not eternal fixtures in God's grand story. God created the institution of marriage for a purpose: for humanity to "be fruitful and multiply" (Genesis 1:28). In the new heavens and new earth, there's no more need to "be fruitful and multiply."

With the mystery of marriage made manifest at the marriage supper of the Lamb (Ephesians 5:32; Revelation 19:6–9), the shadow of earthly marriage will give way to the ultimate reality of Christ being fully united with the church! Our longing for companionship, which may be partially met by marriage (Genesis 2:18–25), will be fully met by God and the true and eternal family of believers.[13]

The absence of marriage and sex doesn't mean that life and relations in the resurrection will be on a level below this present age. Heaven will not consist of an ascetic life of denial. On the contrary, in the consummated life, the elect will be in the fullness of God's glory, worshipping together with the body of Christ and experiencing a much greater kind of existence than anything here and now can compare to. An absence of marriage in heaven communicates that no human relationship can stand even as a momentary flicker before the dazzling brilliance of our awesome and almighty God![14]

I'll say it again: rather than think of singleness as a temporary state before marriage, think of marriage as a temporary state before eternity. The presence of both married and single people in the church reminds us that we're between the ages. As Barry Danylak explains, "Married people are necessary because the church is still part of the current age, but single people remind us that the spiritual age has already been inaugurated in Christ and awaits imminent consummation."[15]

Who Said, "It Is Good"?

The longest sustained discussion in Scripture on singleness is Paul's teaching in 1 Corinthians 7. Paul's words are crucial when examining a biblical theology of singleness. As often is the case, this chapter is not without interpretive challenges, beginning with the second half of verse 1: "Now concerning the matters about which you wrote: 'It is good for a man not to have sexual relations with a woman.'"

Is this statement from Paul or from the Corinthians? The consensus seems to be that the second half of this verse is *not* from Paul; rather, he's quoting from an earlier Corinthian letter. As can be seen, some Bible translations even place quotation marks around this phrase. However, inserting quotation marks is an interpretive decision since this punctuation is not present in the Greek manuscripts.

Those who think these are not Paul's words believe a small group of overzealous Christians were disparaging sexual relations and marriage and Paul needed to correct their extreme asceticism. Much of the argument is based on the supposed implausibility of Paul penning this statement: "It is good for a man not to have sexual relations with a woman."[16]

Why does this matter? If the Corinthians were promoting absolute abstention from sex and marriage, then Paul had to correct this error by encouraging them to marry and enjoy sex in marriage. This is good, right? Certainly, marriage and marital intimacy are good, but this implies that the opposite—chaste singleness in general—is *not* good. But, it's good only for a few who are "called" with the "gift."

Upon further examination, Paul's letter bears little evidence that asceticism was an issue in this fledgling body of believers. The Corinthian believers boasted about incest and patronized prostitutes (5:1; 6:15), and Paul exhorted them to "flee" and "not indulge in sexual immorality"

(6:18; 10:8). Also, this body of believers consisted of many who had been sexually immoral, adulterous, and practicing homosexuality (6:9, 11).

As it turns out, the church at Corinth was predominantly Gentile converts who most likely had yet to fully shed their secular understanding of marriage, sexuality, and singleness.[17] In the Greco-Roman world, prostitutes provided pleasure, while wives simply provided children.

Wives and children were perceived to be a burden. In the first century, marriage and childbearing had gone out of vogue, while men continued to lead lives of debauchery. Some married men would have sex with prostitutes and not their wives, avoiding the responsibility of more legitimate children (7:2–5).[18]

Some have proposed that the sexually immoral and the sexually ascetic worshipped side by side in Corinth.[19] But it's highly unlikely that two diametrically opposite lifestyles could coexist in a moderately sized body of believers.[20] And there's no signal in the text that Paul switched from addressing the sexually immoral group in 1 Corinthians 6 to addressing the sexually ascetic group in 1 Corinthians 7. Furthermore, the use of *porneia* (sexual immorality) in 6:18 and 7:2 suggests continuity rather than discontinuity between the two chapters.

So what was the problem in Corinth? The sexually immoral Corinthians were embracing a secular understanding of sexuality and believing the lie that marriage and children were a burden.[21] Paul encouraged the promiscuous unmarried men to consider marriage—the only proper context for sex (7:2). And he challenged those married—particularly the men who were indulging in extramarital relations and avoiding sex with their wives—to be faithful and stop depriving their spouses of conjugal rights (7:3–5).

In other words, Paul was exhorting the believers in Corinth to holy sexuality—chastity in singleness and faithfulness in marriage. And both are good. But what about the gift that Paul mentions in this chapter? What exactly is it, and what is it not?

A Gift Misunderstood

Gifts are an inseparable part of our lives—birthdays, Christmas, anniversaries, graduations, weddings, babies—the list goes on. Each year we receive a plethora of presents, and if we're honest, we've learned how to assess and rate each one. We keep the good and return or regift the rest. Regrettably, this mind-set has fundamentally warped our understanding of God's gifts.

God has graciously granted believers many undeserved gifts: the Holy Spirit (Acts 2:38; 10:45), justification (Romans 3:24; 5:15–17), eternal life (Romans 6:23), and faith (Ephesians 2:8). In addition, a variety of other gifts are empowered by the Holy Spirit: wisdom, knowledge, faith, healing, miracles, prophecy, discernment, tongues, and interpretation, to name a few (1 Corinthians 12:8–11).

In 1 Corinthians 7:7, Paul—who of course was single—writes this: "I wish that all were as I myself am. But each has his own gift from God, one of one kind and one of another." This may be one of the most misunderstood and disliked gifts from God. What exactly is it? Before answering, let's first ascertain what the gift is *not*. But be prepared. You'll probably be shocked at how much we've misunderstood this gift.

This Gift Is Not a Calling or Vocation

Many understand singleness to be a calling and vocation, based on 1 Corinthians 7, but—perhaps surprisingly—that's incorrect. Allow me to clarify. The word *vocation* has its roots in the Latin *vocatio*, which means "calling." The Greek word translated "call" (*kaleo*) appears nine times in

1 Corinthians 7. When we look specifically at Paul's section on calling, we realize that Paul's use of *call* doesn't refer to a call to singleness but rather denotes the call of salvation.[22]

> Was anyone at the time of his call already circumcised? Let him
> not seek to remove the marks of circumcision. Was anyone at
> the time of his call uncircumcised? Let him not seek circumci-
> sion. For neither circumcision counts for anything nor uncir-
> cumcision, but keeping the commandments of God. Each one
> should remain in the condition in which he was called. Were
> you a bondservant when called? Do not be concerned about it.
> (But if you can gain your freedom, avail yourself of the opportu-
> nity.) For he who was called in the Lord as a bondservant is a
> freedman of the Lord. Likewise he who was free when called is
> a bondservant of Christ. You were bought with a price; do not
> become bondservants of men. So, brothers, in whatever condi-
> tion each was called, there let him remain with God. (verses
> 18–24)

Beyond this call of salvation, a call is generally understood to be something given to only a few special people to fulfill a specific office or duty (Hebrews 5:4). Singleness is not an office or duty. But in 1 Corinthians 7:18–24, Paul writes about being circumcised or uncircumcised, being bond or free. As we can see, these conditions in life are actually quite ordinary and common.

Therefore, in this passage, Paul is not saying that singleness is a unique call or vocation for specially selected people. Then what is Paul trying to communicate when he brings up this *condition* of singleness and the *call* of salvation? The answer is related to my next point.

This Gift Is Not Necessarily Lifelong

Certainly, some devoted and godly Christians receive a special call to lifelong, chaste singleness. However, the singleness discussed in 1 Corinthians 7 is not necessarily one of permanence. It's assumed that verses 17 and 24 refer to lifelong singleness: "Only let each person lead the life that the Lord has assigned to him" and "In whatever condition each was called, there let him remain with God."

Put in context, these verses (7:17–24) come after Paul's discussion of whether a believer should divorce an unbelieving spouse or remain married (verses 12–16). Just as the believer should remain in the condition when saved, she or he should remain married to the unbelieving spouse. The one thing more important than this difficult life condition is the believer's call to salvation.

Paul is not commanding singles to be forever locked in their unmarried state but saying their conversion to Christ has totally eclipsed it. God's call of salvation makes any felt need to change one's condition—married or unmarried, circumcised or uncircumcised, bond or free—essentially irrelevant.[23]

Most think 1 Corinthians 7 contains Paul's teaching on *celibacy*. Richard Sipe, author of many books on celibacy, defines it as a chosen, lifelong vocation of abstention from marriage and sex.[24] However, in 1 Corinthians 7, singleness is not a special call or vocation. Neither is Paul exhorting people to commit to lifelong singleness.

The majority of Christian singles I know are not called to lifelong celibacy, yet they find themselves in the more common *unchosen* state of singleness. My hope is to address this phenomenon, which is why I prefer to use *singleness* (chosen or unchosen state) rather than *celibacy* (chosen vocation). In addition, the term *singleness* most closely represents the Greek word *agamos* ("unmarried") used by Paul throughout 1 Corinthians 7.

Many assume that lifelong celibacy is the only option for believers with same-sex attractions. While we shouldn't promote biblical marriage as the ultimate prize (as ex-gay ministries have done in the past), we also shouldn't discount the possibility that God can do the improbable.

Mandating lifelong celibacy for those with same-sex attractions on the false premise that biblical marriage is impossible for them does not permit God to be God—the only One who determines the future. There's nothing wrong in praying that God will provide for us a spouse. But we should learn from Jesus when he prayed in the Garden of Gethsemane, "Nevertheless, not my will, but yours, be done" (Luke 22:42).

It's best for us singles to live with an open hand and allow God to assign our life condition according to his infinite wisdom and abounding love for us.

This Gift Is Not a Special Capacity for Enjoying Singleness

I often hear the following explanation regarding the gift of singleness: if a person is happy being single, then he has the gift; if she wants to marry, then she doesn't have the gift.[25] This reduces God's gift to a subjective feeling or desire.[26] A desire for a gift doesn't mean one has it, nor does an aversion to a gift mean one doesn't have it. Human emotions can't be the determining factor for any gift from God.

Paul explains in Ephesian 2:8 that faith is a gift from God. When saints are being persecuted for their faith and suffering for the sake of Christ, are happy emotions the arbiter of their great faith? Also, God's gift should not be viewed as a way to avoid suffering in order to be happy. Prophecy is also a gift (Romans 12:6), yet many prophets of old experienced much suffering and heartbreak. God is concerned less about our happiness and more about our holiness.

This Gift Is Not Continence

One commentator states, "An active libido is simply a sign that celibacy is not for them."[27] This implies that only a few with the gift of continence are able to practice self-control, while everyone else is unable to resist sexual temptations and must marry.

But fleeing sexual temptation is not a unique or selective gift from God. The Holy Spirit abides in all believers and is the cause and means by which sin is mortified.[28] Even married people must put to death illicit sexual temptations. Self-control is not a spiritual gift but a sign of Christian maturity (Galatians 5:23).

Is marriage the remedy for a man or woman with a severe pornography addiction? Too many have taken Paul's words out of context: "It is better to marry than to burn with passion" (1 Corinthians 7:9). The Corinthians were spurning marriage while engaging in extramarital sex, and Paul chastised their lack of self-control and motivated them to consider marriage as a good option.

When speaking to high school and college kids, I often tell the young ladies that if their boyfriend wants to marry as soon as possible because he doesn't want to "burn with passion," they should run as fast as possible away from a man so lacking in self-control. The same is true for boyfriends being pressured by their girlfriends to quickly marry in order to have sex. Wanting to have sex is not the right reason to marry.

A correct reason to marry should be when a young man is willing to give himself up for his future wife, as Christ did for the church (Ephesians 5:25), or when a young woman realizes that being united with her future husband will bring great glory to God and exponentially amplify their effectiveness together to reflect and proclaim the gospel. Simply put, a lack of self-control *before* marriage means a lack of self-control *in* marriage.

This Gift Is Not a Spiritual Gift

Paul writes in 1 Corinthians 7:7, "Each has his own gift from God." Several words in the New Testament convey the meaning of "gift"; two common words are *doron* and *dorea*. However, in this verse the apostle uses a different word: *charisma,* derived from the Greek word for "grace," *charis*—thus, "grace-gift."[29]

Paul uses this same word to describe spiritual gifts such as prophecy, teaching, miracles, and healing (Romans 12:6–8; 1 Corinthians 12:8–11, 28–31). In the past, I thought this gift in 1 Corinthians 7:7 meant spiritual gift. Upon further investigation, I was surprised at what I found.

When Paul begins his discussion in 1 Corinthians 12 on spiritual gifts, he makes it clear that he isn't talking about normal gifts; rather, these are spiritual matters (*pneumatikos*). In addition, these spiritual gifts are unlike other gifts in that they are empowered by and are manifestations of the Holy Spirit (verses 6–7). However, in reference to the gift in 1 Corinthians 7, Paul makes no mention of the Holy Spirit.

Also, the spiritual gifts in 1 Corinthians 12 are *functional*—each one accomplishes a specific task or ministry unique to itself. The gift of prophecy accomplishes the task of prophesying, the gift of teaching accomplishes the task of teaching, and so on. Singleness, however, accomplishes no unique ministry task; in the church, singles can generally perform most if not all of the same ministry functions that married people can.[30]

So if this gift in 1 Corinthians 7:7 is not a vocation, a lifelong condition, enjoyment, continence, or a spiritual gift, then what is it? It's simply a gift from God—in other words, singleness is just good. There is no need to read more into it.

A Simple Gift

In Romans 6:23, Paul says, "The wages of sin is death, but the free gift of God is eternal life in Christ Jesus our Lord." Paul in that verse writes that eternal life is a *charisma,* the same word used in 1 Corinthians 7:7. Eternal life is not a calling to a specific task but an objective status of having been "set free from sin" (Romans 6:22).

Also, in Romans 5:16, Paul says, "The free gift is not like the result of that one man's sin. For the judgment following one trespass brought condemnation, but the free gift following many trespasses brought justification." The *charisma* here is justification. This is an objective status of being credited with Christ's own righteousness.

These two gifts—eternal life and justification—are given not to only a few Christians but to all who have received the call of salvation. Although these gifts are of inexpressible worth, they aren't "special" in the sense that only a few believers have them.

This gift mentioned by Paul in 1 Corinthians 7:7 doesn't need to be overspiritualized, and we shouldn't make the text say more than it says. Quite simply, singleness is a gift. It is good—nothing special, nothing complicated, nothing out of the ordinary. It may be that Paul intentionally doesn't expound on this gift *because there isn't much to explain.*

Singleness is simply a gift that is good. When we think singleness is some special spiritual gift, we keep searching for aspects of singleness or special abilities that somehow magnify it. Paul may just be saying that singleness, in and of itself, is good.

Remember again Paul's statement in that verse: "Each has his own gift from God, one of one kind and one of another." Albert Hsu, author of *Singles at the Crossroads,* explains that Paul's words here seem to communicate two mutually exclusive gifts. He concludes that Paul is communicating that singleness is a gift and marriage is a gift—both are good!

One isn't better or worse than the other. As a matter of fact, the view that singleness is some "special" gift creates a false two-tier system for unmarried people: those possessing the special gift of singleness are more spiritual; those without it must wait around to get married.[31]

The reality is that most will marry. But at any given time, some will be single—as never married, widowed, or divorced. Singleness is a gift for everyone at least once in life. As Paul outlines, whatever our life condition—married, unmarried, circumcised, uncircumcised, bond, or free—the thing of ultimate importance is our call of salvation, which makes the potential difficulties of any life condition essentially moot.

Some pastors have approached me and expressed concern about my emphasis on the goodness of singleness. They believe it reflects a worldly mind-set that denigrates marriage and celebrates the free-living noncommitment associated with singleness.

These leaders often grieve the abundance of young single men in the church who are irresponsible, immature, and fearful of commitment. These pastors strongly advocate for marriage and family. They believe the solution must be to make these young men stop running from responsibility and get married.

I also lament that too many young men in our churches are irresponsible, immature, and fearful of commitment. And I agree that the world's celebration of secular singleness—namely, reckless serial dating and premarital sex—is not only incorrect but also sinful. However, I don't believe the primary solution is to make these young men marry as soon as possible. That could be a disaster.

What these young men need is to be born again. And if they claim to be Christian, they need to be mentored and challenged to become godly and mature disciples. The problem really isn't singleness. The problem is the failure to be a real follower of Jesus Christ and to be a true man or woman of God.

Being single is a gift, and being married is a gift. Just as salvation is understood as a good gift from God, both singleness and marriage are good gifts from God. How can this be? Being unmarried is a gift simply because of our glorious and wonderful call to Christ—our undeserved call of salvation!

If you're single, then in light of these truths you can know that your singleness is a gift from God. And what does singleness mean as a gift from God? Paul explains that being single frees us from certain anxieties so that we may "please the Lord" (1 Corinthians 7:32).

Singleness allows us to give "undivided devotion to the Lord" (verse 35)—if we so choose. Just as marriage done well gives glory to God, singleness done well also gives glory to God. The real issue is not whether you have the gift but whether you realize singleness to *be* good and *for* your good. Singleness is an opportunity to love Christ and serve his church with undivided devotion.

Understanding singleness as a gift means you don't have to be special or uniquely called to know the state of singleness is good. Also, you can have the gift of singleness and have a desire to marry. The gift of singleness doesn't necessarily mean it's lifelong. Nor does it mean it'll be easy or you'll always be happy. It will be difficult, just as being married brings trials! However, trials and difficulties don't diminish the goodness of either.

Living out singleness as a gift doesn't mean you won't struggle with sexual temptations or with loneliness. They're both a reality of life, not just for the single woman or man. Paul's main message in 1 Corinthians 7 is that whatever life condition we find ourselves in, whether married or unmarried, it's our call of salvation—our call to Christ—that matters most. This reality must be our daily anchor through every storm of life.

14

SPIRITUAL FAMILY

Everlasting Brotherhood and Sisterhood

If you were a teenager in the 1980s, you're more than likely familiar with the movie *Stand by Me*. It's a coming-of-age story set in rural Oregon. Four boys set out on a hike to find a missing boy who went picking blueberries and was most likely hit and killed by a train.

The movie begins with an adult Gordie, the main character, reading a newspaper article about his childhood best friend, Chris. Chris was fatally stabbed in a fast-food restaurant while attempting to break up a fight. Narrated by Gordie, the whole movie is a flashback to Labor Day weekend in 1959 and the life-defining adventure of these four young friends.

In the last scene, it's revealed that Gordie, now a successful author, is writing out this nostalgic account. On the old 1980s-style computer screen, he types the last few sentences reflecting on his old buddy Chris.

He was stabbed in the throat. He died almost instantly. Although I hadn't seen him in more than ten years, I know I'll miss him forever. I never had any friends later on like the ones I had when I was twelve . . . does anyone?[1]

There is something innocent and pure about childhood friendships—before love interests and romances came along and deprioritized these special types of bonds. At that age, our hearts were on our sleeves, and we had all the time in the world for each other. Secret handshakes. Best-friend-forever vows. There's a sense of idealism and beauty in this youthful camaraderie.

In light of holy sexuality—chastity in singleness and faithfulness in marriage—many of us with same-sex attractions still find ourselves unmarried while longing to experience the joy of a committed relationship. Although marriage is not the cure for loneliness, we still have a legitimate desire for intimacy and community. What's the best way to meet these needs? Should we look for a spiritual "best friend forever"? Is the answer to seek out a covenant friendship as long as we both shall live and until death do us part?

It's next to impossible to measure the value of a good friend. God blesses us with these life-giving relationships to edify and grow us. Like other blessings, we must steward these gifts well. Although same-sex-attracted individuals must parse out sinful sexual and romantic desires—as everyone else does—longings for healthy, platonic same-sex friendships should not be feared or suppressed. God has given us all a healthy desire for same-sex friendships.

Unfortunately, men have been conditioned to believe that any intimacy or affection toward another man is a sign of weakness—or that they're gay. In the 1980s LA Lakers star Magic Johnson and Detroit Pistons guard Isiah Thomas would embrace at half court with a kiss on the cheek before playing. Not surprisingly, many called them gay. It's a tragic sign of our times that we have diminished and demeaned healthy same-sex friendships. Grown men are no longer able to show affection to other men, as if love and intimacy are reserved for marriage and sex only.

Many Christian men are deathly afraid to build a godly friendship with a same-sex-attracted Christian brother for fear that it might become inappropriate. I'm so grateful for the great brothers in the Lord who have boldly and intimately walked with me in my journey toward our Savior. I needed to relearn how to love other men in the way God intended—not in sexual or romantic ways but in ways that honor God and help me die to myself daily.

So how does the Bible express a healthy, God-honoring relationship that is not sexual or romantic?

The Bible and Relationships

The concept of friendship is mentioned in a few places in Scripture. Abraham is called a friend of God (2 Chronicles 20:7; Isaiah 41:8; James 2:23). King Solomon spoke highly of friendship: "A friend loves at all times" (Proverbs 17:17). He even compared a friend with family: "There is a friend who sticks closer than a brother" (Proverbs 18:24). On the night before his crucifixion, Jesus told his disciples, "You are my friends if you do what I command you. No longer do I call you servants . . . but I have called you friends" (John 15:14–15).

David and Jonathan's relationship is one of the most celebrated bonds of companionship between two men in the Bible. Some gay activists have erroneously attempted to eroticize their love.[2] These activists will point to 2 Samuel 1:26 in which Jonathan's affection for David is described as "surpassing the love of women." But just because two men love each other does not necessarily mean they're lovers. Besides, it's quite obvious from the biblical record that David's issue was not men but women!

It's regrettable today that love between two men often means nothing other than a same-sex sexual or romantic relationship. Can't two men deeply love each other without others assuming they're gay? Is love really equivalent to sex? How many people do you know that are having sex and don't actually love each other? No matter what the world says, love does *not* equal sex.

The loyalty of David and Jonathan was certainly special and selfless, bound by "a covenant before the Lord" (1 Samuel 23:18). But what sort of covenant was this? Evidence shows that it couldn't have been a marital covenant, as gay activists purport. Robert Gagnon, author of *The Bible and Homosexual Practice,* convincingly explains that the covenant between David and Jonathan wasn't marriage but had both a sociopolitical and a familial aspect.

It wasn't uncommon for two political leaders of approximately equal power to express love for each other. King Hiram of Tyre "always loved David" (1 Kings 5:1). In addition, Jonathan took off his robe and armor and gave them to David, along with "even his sword and his bow and his belt" (1 Samuel 18:4). This expression of admiration, affection, and loyalty symbolized the voluntary transference of the heir-apparent status from Jonathan to David.[3]

This covenanted relationship was also an expression of familial love and commitment. David calls his deceased friend "my brother Jonathan" (2 Samuel 1:26). Also, in 1 Samuel 18:1, "the soul of Jonathan was knit to the soul of David." This distinct expression of a "soul knit to a soul" is found in the Bible one other time. In Genesis 44:30, Judah says that his father's soul (Jacob) is knit to his youngest brother's soul (Benjamin)— "his life is bound up in the boy's life." This expression communicates a strong form of love between two family members.

Although the sociopolitical aspect is present in David and Jonathan's relationship, it's obvious their association went beyond mere power, status, or alliance. They were great friends, even best friends. However, interestingly, the term *friend* is notably absent in the narrative texts about David and Jonathan, and the New Testament does not mention their idealized friendship.

This doesn't imply that they weren't friends—they certainly were! But maybe the biblical writers didn't intend for us to idealize it. Instead,

Scripture communicates that their relationship was more than friendship. Jonathan requests this of David: "If I am still alive, show me the steadfast love of the LORD, that I may not die; and do not cut off your steadfast love from my house forever" (1 Samuel 20:14–15).

This love was not simply between two men but also between two houses now fused together by their covenant. In other words, David and Jonathan were a new *family;* they were best friends and the closest of *brothers.* The reason Scripture doesn't further expound on friendship could be that God has already established something greater and more enduring.

We Are Family

Without substantial attention on friendship, the Old Testament places an explicit emphasis on family and blood relatives. For the ancient Israelite, personal identity was tied to kinship with three major concentric circles: house, clan, and tribe.[4] Often the most trusted and intimate relationships in the Old Testament were family members and blood relatives.

Then in the New Testament, Jesus provides some strong words about familial relationships. For example, he says in Matthew 10:35–37 (Luke 14:26–27),

I have come to set a man against his father, and a daughter against her mother, and a daughter-in-law against her mother-in-law. And a person's enemies will be those of his own household. Whoever loves father or mother more than me is not worthy of me, and whoever loves son or daughter more than me is not worthy of me.

Two chapters later in the same gospel, Jesus's mother and brothers go to Jesus. When told his family wanted to speak to him, he replies, "Who is my mother, and who are my brothers?" (Matthew 12:48; Mark 3:33; Luke 8:20–21). Is Jesus breaking from the Old Testament and declaring that families are no longer good?

The answer is found when Jesus points to his disciples and says, "Here are my mother and my brothers! For whoever does the will of my Father in heaven is my brother and sister and mother" (Matthew 12:49–50). Jesus is not rejecting family; instead, he is elevating something even greater than blood family and friends—that is, "spiritual family." In other words, the bonds of *spiritual family* run deeper than those of blood family and friends.

Families that consist of a husband, wife, and children are really momentary blessings of this age only. In the consummated age to come, the family of the redeemed—the church—will continue into eternity, forever and ever! In *This Momentary Marriage*, John Piper puts it best: "I am declaring the temporary and secondary nature of marriage and family over against the eternal and primary nature of the church."[5] What a glorious picture of the consummated body of Christ!

To all who are in Christ, this concept of *spiritual family* arises naturally out of God's grand story—creation, fall, redemption, and consummation. In Christ, a new community is being built. A community bound not by blood relations (houses, clans, and tribes) or even by marital vows. A community of Jew and Gentile, married and single, male and female, young and old, opposite-sex attracted and same-sex attracted. This new community is the church of the redeemed, the true and eternal family of God bound by the blood of the Lamb!

Entrance into this new family is not through physical birth but through spiritual *rebirth*. The mission of the community under the old covenant was being a part of a physical family and having physical children. But the mission of the new community under the new covenant is being a part of the spiritual family and producing spiritual children—making disciples and expanding the kingdom of God.[6]

Being Adopted by Father God

Scriptural support for covenanted and vowed friendship is present but sparse. However, the depth and breadth of biblical evidence for spiritual family is overwhelming, and it all begins with the fatherhood of God and our adoption.

The occurrences of God as Father in the Old Testament are relatively few, only about fourteen.[7] However, *Father* is Jesus's favorite term when addressing God. In the Synoptic Gospels (Matthew, Mark, and Luke), "Father" is spoken by Jesus sixty-five times, and in John, over a hundred times. Although the Gospels translate nearly all Jesus's words into the Greek word for father, *pater,* in Mark 14:36 the word remains in Aramaic, *Abba,* which is an endearing and intimate word children used to refer to their father.[8]

For Paul, the fatherhood of God is what ties together the core doctrines of redemption and adoption. In Galatians 4:4–6, Paul writes, "When the fullness of time had come, God sent forth his Son, born of woman, born under the law, to redeem those who were under the law, so that we might receive adoption as sons. And because you are sons, God has sent the Spirit of his Son into our hearts, crying, 'Abba! Father!'"

As Christians, we celebrate our redemption, but too often we just stop there. Paul tells us in the passage above that the *purpose* of redemption was "so that we might receive adoption as sons." Thus, the concept of spiritual family is grounded in adoption, the result of redemption. If we are truly redeemed, then God is our Father. If we are truly children of

God, then we are one spiritual family *eternally* tied together as brothers and sisters in Christ.

Reclaiming True Brotherhood and Sisterhood

Today we have limited the deepest and most intimate form of love to marriage. Christians are called to love everyone, but we rank the depth of intimacy from marriage at the top, then family, then church, and others at the bottom. Joseph Hellerman, author of *When the Church Was a Family,* studied the Mediterranean world of antiquity and found that primary allegiance was to family and that sibling relationships even took precedence over spouses.[9] In addition, Jesus's words on family communicate that he intends believers to function as family.

Therefore, *brother* was the early Christians' key term of intimacy and community in the body of Christ. The Greek word for "brother" or "sister" is *adelphos,* which is found nearly 350 times in the New Testament. For us Christians today, "brother" and "sister" must actually mean something, and it should be a lived-out reality in our daily lives.

If relationships can be ranked, Christians should see only two major categories: God's family and others. A wife is first a daughter of God. Being a wife is of this world only, while being a child of God is eternal. This is why a believer must not marry an unbeliever—it's the wrong family. Within the body of Christ, we can still have "best" brother or sister relationships. But the context is still the church.

There is no need to create a new form of relationship as a better mode of intimacy and companionship, such as a covenanted "spiritual" friendship. Friendship is not meant to be over-sentimentalized, nor is it meant to replace marriage. The New Testament has already created a new community through which our primary needs for companionship and intimacy can be met. Yet the problem is that we really aren't living as family. We aren't living as true spiritual brothers and sisters in Christ, and as a result, many singles—particularly those with same-sex attractions—experience feelings of confinement and isolation.

This feeling of confinement is largely due to the simple fact that we've lost the profound meaning and depth of spiritual family, of brothers and sisters in Christ. The ultimate answer to our deepest longings is found not in another person or a support group disconnected from the church but in Christ and in his body.

The Christian life is always about a healthy tension, and that's true in the arena of our relationships as well. In the midst of guarding our hearts from desires that ultimately cannot please God, we must boldly and lavishly pursue brotherly and sisterly bonds in the family of God. If we're all cleansed and united by the blood of Christ, then let's really live like it. If we truly began living as brothers and sisters in Christ, the problem of loneliness would most likely begin fading away.

I grieve that shallow and short-lived friendships are so often the norm and not the unacceptable, especially among men. I really appreciate the efforts to challenge the myth that committed relational intimacy is found *only* in marriage. Does this mean that because all believers are brothers and sisters, the level of intimacy will be the same for everyone? Is it inappropriate to have a tighter bond with a couple of brothers or sisters? It's natural within every family to grow particularly close with certain members and to have a closest brother or sister.

Just by sheer volume of passages, the Bible shows that spiritual brotherhood or sisterhood is what relationships look like for the redeemed community. So what is the difference between having a "best brother" and having a "best friend"? The spiritual family—that is, the church—involves inherent family benefits that aren't inherent in friendship.

Inherent Family Benefits

One of the main reasons I include this chapter on spiritual family is because of the growing trend of Christians believing that involvement in the local church—our *spiritual* family—is unnecessary. They will often justify their stance like this: "I have close Christian friends. Going to church doesn't make you a Christian. The church is not a building, but it's people. My Christian friends and I *are* the church, so we don't need to go to church."

This can be dangerous and disastrous for anybody—including individuals with same-sex attractions. These men and women may experience intimacy and commitment with their Christian friends but are isolated from true family. Being untethered from a local church is being untethered from Christ. How can we have union with Christ if we don't have union with the body of Christ?

Christian friends are essential and can provide godly counsel. But they can also provide poor counsel, especially when separated from the wisdom and accountability of the people of God. Solomon's son Rehoboam listened to his imprudent friends, and this led to the breakup of the united kingdom. "But [Rehoboam] abandoned the counsel that the old men gave him and took counsel with the young men who had grown up with him and stood before him" (1 Kings 12:8).

Job lost everything, but his three friends went and sat with him on the ground for seven days and seven nights. While mourning together, they spoke no words (Job 2:13). Sadly, trouble came when Eliphaz, Bildad, and Zophar opened their mouths. The rest of the book consists mostly of their poor advice to Job and Job's defense. In the end, God rebuked these three friends for their folly (42:7–8).

Christian friends are *part* of the body of Christ, but we cannot say they *are* the body of Christ or can replace it! So what's the difference between a regular and intentional gathering of Christian friends and the regular and intentional gathering of the local church? Aren't these two basically the same? No, they are fundamentally different in at least three important ways: the preaching of God's Word, the sacraments or ordinances, and headship.

The Preaching of God's Word

I don't know of any friends who regularly hang out together and actually preach to one another. They may talk *about* God's Word, but this is different from the public proclamation of God's Word. The reading, teaching, and preaching of Scripture are inherent aspects of the local body of Christ.

When ancient Israel gathered, the leaders publicly read Scripture to the people of God (Exodus 24:7; Joshua 8:34; 2 Kings 23:2; Nehemiah 8:8). The first-century church continued this practice of publicly reading God's Word (Colossians 4:16; 1 Thessalonians 5:27; 1 Timothy 4:13).

In his first letter to Timothy, Paul provides some instructions on the worship gatherings of the local body of believers in Ephesus. He exhorts Timothy to be devoted to the public reading and teaching of Scripture and to exhortation (1 Timothy 4:13). In his last-known letter to Timothy, the apostle reminds his disciple, "Preach the word; be ready in season and out of season" (2 Timothy 4:2).

The preaching of God's Word is one of the main things that separates the local church from a gathering of Christians. It helps believers stay anchored in correct doctrine and away from false teaching. But how is this different from going to a conference where the Word of God is being preached? The local church also baptizes converts and administers the Lord's Supper (the sacraments and ordinances).

Baptism and the Lord's Supper

The ordinances or sacraments of baptism and the Lord's Supper are specific to the church. The only form of covenanted relationships that the New Testament conveys is one shaped by God's grand story: spiritual brotherhood and sisterhood. The redeemed are family with baptism as the initial sign of the covenant and the Lord's Supper as the ongoing affirmation of this covenant.

We are baptized in the name of the Father, the Son, and the Holy Spirit (Matthew 28:19). Baptism also unites us with Christ in his death and resurrection (Romans 6:3–5). We regularly receive the Lord's Supper to remember and "proclaim the Lord's death until he comes" (1 Corinthians 11:26). The local body of believers baptizes and partakes of the Lord's Supper as a way of "covenanting" together as the family of God.

But again, what is the difference between two covenanted best friends and the family of God? Not only is the Word of God not regularly preached, but two best friends also don't constitute the body of Christ under spiritual headship, where discipleship, accountability, discipline, and restoration are inherent aspects.

Headship and the Body

The body of Christ has many members. Paul explains, "For the body does not consist of one member but of many" (1 Corinthians 12:14). A body has a head, and the head of the body is Christ himself (Colossians 1:18). The body is also made up of church leaders who guide and shepherd the flock as pastors (Ephesians 4:11–12).

While best friends can tend to be more inward focused and sometimes isolated, spiritual family should be both inward and outward focused. As brothers and sisters, we are tethered to the local church and under its spiritual authority. This accountability helps foster healthy relationships that aren't segregated from the body of believers.

Our pastors, elders, and church leaders must be present in our lives. But this occurs only if we include them and allow them to speak wisdom and truth to us. In essence, this is discipleship. Although discipleship involves a strong friendship between mentor and disciple, friendship is not equivalent to discipleship. The ideal context for discipleship is the local church.

Accountability for both encouragement and correction is a key aspect in the life of every Christian, but it involves work and risk. Fortunately, accountability is inherent in a healthy church. Jesus lays the framework of accountability and discipline, both of which are family responsibilities:

> If your brother sins against you, go and tell him his fault, between
> you and him alone. If he listens to you, you have gained your
> brother. But if he does not listen, take one or two others along
> with you, that every charge may be established by the evidence of
> two or three witnesses. If he refuses to listen to them, tell it to the
> church. And if he refuses to listen even to the church, let him be
> to you as a Gentile and a tax collector. (Matthew 18:15–17)

In verses 21–22, we learn that not only are accountability and discipline inherent in spiritual family but forgiveness and restoration are as well. Peter asks, "Lord, how often will my brother sin against me, and I forgive him? As many as seven times?" Jesus answers him, "I do not say to you seven times, but seventy-seven times." Discipline must always be done with the intent of restoration and forgiveness (2 Corinthians 2:5–11; Galatians 6:1).

Regrettably, church discipline is often ignored or, when applied, seems more retributive in nature than filled with the hope of a redemptive restoration. Especially for those guilty of sexual sin, a lot of shame, isolation, and fear are involved. Biblical restoration after a moral fall is essentially a family reunion where the prodigal comes back from a far country and is again one with the body of Christ.

Are we doing family well? Is this a lived-out reality? The church isn't as healthy as it should be. We have much to improve in this area because we aren't truly acting as we ought. If we really lived as spiritual family, as true brothers and sisters in Christ, I believe we could effectively mitigate issues like loneliness and isolation, along with the sorrow and pain that often accompany them.

Relationships with our brothers or sisters in Christ should be among the most intimate and real relationships we have. One-flesh union of husband and wife makes it unique compared with other relationships. Yet it is still a temporary union for our time on earth. The only permanent human relationship is between those bound by Christ's blood in the spiritual family of God.

However, we must say this: friendship is not meant to replace marriage, and marriage is not meant to replace friendship. The reason why we do not need a covenant best friend is simply because God has given us covenant brothers and sisters in the body of Christ. This doesn't mean that you'll be close to all in the same way—we will have closer brothers or sisters. In the same way, marriage is not meant to replace the godly same-sex sibling relationships we must cultivate as we follow Jesus together!

The key to a healthy and intimate spiritual family is integration. This should be inherent in the local church, but it isn't always the case. If we indeed lived as family, we wouldn't be so segregated. There's a place for more narrowly focused fellowship groups, but a healthy church is an integrated church. The church as family affirms that life together is necessary and beneficial for all—same-sex attracted or opposite-sex attracted, single or married.

We learn and grow from one another. A single person can learn so much from a married individual, and vice versa. The same applies to age differences as well. Why are our youth not learning from some of our older saints? And why are young couples not learning from some of the godly, single elderly women and men in our congregations?

In the relational voids that are common in churches, many Christians with same-sex attractions want to find a friend just like them who can completely understand their situation. But maybe this isn't part of God's plan. Why do we need to find someone *just like us*? I know that it's more comfortable and it's easier. But God wants to stretch and grow us. It's more challenging to develop brotherhood or sisterhood with someone very different, but it brings great reward.

My best friend, Joe Hendrickson, is a true brother in the Lord. We were roommates at Moody Bible Institute, and he now serves as an associate pastor in the Spokane area. Our brotherhood has continued to this day. Honestly, we're quite different. He loves the outdoors, and I would rather stay inside. He's excellent at every sport, and I can barely catch a ball. I'm an extrovert, and he's an introvert. But we both love the Lord.

Joe is one of the most honest and transparent young men I know, a man who passionately loves the Lord and wants him to be known. It's because of our differences, not in spite of them, that I've tremendously grown through our relationship to love Jesus more. If I were looking for someone just like me, I would never have had this close brother relationship.

Again, my fear with focusing too much on a best friend, especially one who's just like me, is that I'll miss out on the diversity of the family of God and all it means. If we're family, then nuclear families won't treat singles like outsiders. The homes of families would have singles in them who aren't "physical" family. However, married people must take the initiative.

It's much harder—and sometimes inappropriate—for a single person to invite himself into the life and home of a family. But it's completely appropriate for a husband and wife to invite a single sister or brother into the regular life of the couple's home. I dream of the day when this becomes a reality. Imagine the message a married couple conveys when they give their single friend a house key and say, "Come whenever you want. We *are* family!"[10]

I cannot stress too much how crucial spiritual family is for singles—particularly those with the "double curse" of having same-sex attractions. We have no family of our own. No spouse to hold when we lie in bed. No kids to return to after a rough and tiring day. For many, it's just an empty, dark, and cold apartment.

Spiritual family means that if the church were actually the church, if the body of Christ were actually the body of Christ, if the family of God were actually the family of God, then *not* having a physical family wouldn't really matter! Because we'd have *real* family. A family that is eternal. I'd have spiritual brothers and sisters to hold me and comfort me and love me and point me to Christ.

Will you commit to making this a reality for the sake of me and all Christian singles? More importantly, will you do it for the sake of Christ, by making the beauty and glory of his body known? "By this all people will know that you are my disciples, if you have love for one another" (John 13:35).

15

SANCTIFICATION

The Path to Holy Sexuality

Michelangelo was one of the greatest artists of the Italian High Renaissance. Few match his versatility as a sculptor, painter, architect, and poet. Michelangelo was born into a family of minor nobility, and because the arts were deemed unworthy of their social position, Michelangelo's father initially discouraged the young man from pursuing art. However, this prodigy didn't give up, and he soon became a young and distinguished artist.

Michelangelo's mother wasn't healthy and passed away when he was only six. When Michelangelo was a baby, the family hired a wet nurse to care for him. The nurse's husband and father were both stonemasons, and the hills northeast of Florence had many rock quarries. As an adult, Michelangelo told a friend in jest that all his artistic ability came from "the pure air of your native Arezzo, and also because I sucked in chisels and hammers with my nurse's milk."[1]

Michelangelo viewed himself primarily as a sculptor, and his most prominent stone masterpiece is *David*. Before he began chiseling, Michelangelo was known to create a smaller wax model of the planned statue. He then submerged the model in water and slowly raised it; the master sculptor carefully studied from the top down what he saw slowly emerging.[2] For the seventeen-foot statute of David, Michelangelo probably pictured the complete form held within the immense block of white marble, then simply hammered out everything that wasn't David.

Every good artist not only must visualize her or his end goal but also must comprehend the process to achieve it. The means is just as important as the end. No process, no product. If Michelangelo's procedures were incorrect, there would be no masterpiece.

The same is true for the Christian life. Not surprisingly, God has revealed to us in his Word what our final state and process should look like. God exhorts us in the Old Testament and again in the New, "Be holy, for I am holy" (Leviticus 11:44–45; 1 Peter 1:16). Holiness is the goal, and sanctification is the process.

Unfortunately, many Christians have envisioned an incorrect goal and a faulty process for those of us with same-sex attractions. I've explained in this book how everyone's goal in regard to sexuality should be *holy* sexuality—chastity in singleness and faithfulness in marriage.

For too many and for too long, holy sexuality has not been the goal, and singleness has been deprecated. Unmarried Christians are projects to be "fixed," so we try to "fix" them up with someone. Think about the words we use. Although we have made some progress in recognizing that the correct objective is holy sexuality, not heterosexuality, many still embrace the wrong process by continuing to use "sexual-orientation change" therapy as their main methodology.

I'm often asked, "Do you still have same-sex attractions?" Sometimes people ask it in a different way: "Have you been fully delivered?" Queries like these stem from a sincere desire to better understand me and my journey of coming to faith and of following Jesus on a daily basis. I love helping a fellow brother or sister better understand the topic of sexuality. Yet behind these questions is a misunderstanding of what the process of sanctification looks like for all the redeemed.

After Paul's list of vices in 1 Corinthians 6:9–10, which includes same-sex sexual behavior, he says this: "Such were some of you" (verse 11). Later, in a different epistle, Paul makes a stark distinction between the believer's preconversion and postconversion realities: "The old has passed away; behold, the new has come" (2 Corinthians 5:17).

But if a Christian—who is a new creation—is still tempted with same-sex sexual desires, does that mean no true transformation, no real healing, and no complete deliverance have occurred? Does conversion mean that same-sex attractions should be a thing of the past? Or more generally, is the Christian's goal while here on earth the eradication of trials and temptations?

Let me offer an illustration. Beau was a drunk, but by God's saving grace, he has become a Christian and stopped drinking. However, even after years of sobriety, he admits he still has urges to drink—but he doesn't. Would we therefore question Beau's transformation? Would we doubt that he's been healed? Does Beau need further deliverance? Does Beau need the demon of alcoholism cast out of him? No!

In fact, the manifestation of God's grace is more evident in his life because he says no to his flesh and says yes to Christ! It's when we live holy, even in the midst of temptations, that God is glorified.

In an earlier chapter, I discussed temptation's reality, how temptations are not sinful per se but can certainly lead to sin. Then what does daily life look like for the ordinary Christian who is tempted? From the point of our conversion until at last we enter the presence of the Lord, what's the process for our pursuit of holiness?

And in particular—because of this book's focus on holy sexuality— what does it mean to *be holy* and to *become holy* for people like myself who may experience same-sex attractions? Let's begin by further exploring the doctrine of sanctification and by dispelling certain myths about it.

What Is Sanctification?

Sanctification is grounded in the essential character of God. The prophet Isaiah, at the beginning of his ministry, received a vision in which he saw the Lord seated on a throne, while the seraphim above declared, *"Holy, holy, holy* is the LORD of hosts; the whole earth is full of his glory!" (Isaiah 6:3, emphasis added). This threefold verbal repetition represents the strongest superlative in the Hebrew language.

In the Old Testament, holiness was juxtaposed with things that were common (Leviticus 10:10). Being sanctified meant to be set apart from the ordinary to be used by God. Objects in the temple were set apart for a specific purpose established by the Lord. The people of Israel were called to be a holy nation set apart from the world (Exodus 19:6; Leviticus 20:26). Similarly, in the New Testament, Jewish and Gentile believers were set apart and chosen as "a holy nation" (1 Peter 2:9).

Because of who he is, the one true God and Creator is set apart from all false gods as well as from all creation. In the ancient Near Eastern world, the character of the local deity determined the character of its worshippers.[3] As heathens practiced indiscriminate sex and even sacrificed their own children, they were reflecting the morality of their pagan gods, such as Baal, Asherah, and Molech.

However, the Lord our God is righteous, does not delight in wickedness, and hates evil (Psalm 11:7; 5:4; Zechariah 8:17). He therefore requires of his people, "Be holy, for I am holy" (Leviticus 11:45; 1 Peter 1:16). And sanctification is God's expressed will for our lives (1 Thessalonians 4:3).

A morally upright deity with a divine expectation for his worshippers' ethical behavior was truly unique in the ancient world. In this, Judaism and Christianity are set apart from all other ancient religions. As a child of God, I'm daily called to reflect the holy nature of the God I worship.

As Christians, we must pursue righteousness and resist evil. No one questions this. Yet the easy mistake is to turn the process of sanctification into simply following a set of rules: do right, and don't do wrong. Spiritual maturity has become merely a pursuit of moral virtue. For the individual who experiences same-sex attractions, is holy sexuality achieved by rigorous willpower, self-discipline, and behavior modification?

Our skewed understanding of Christian holiness often looks more like works-righteousness than anything flowing from our triune God. Sanctification cannot be achieved by sheer human effort because only God can sanctify. Although we must strive to do right, this does nothing to conquer our sinful nature that keeps us from righteousness. Instead of slavishly laboring to achieve moral virtue, we must grasp the important concept that Puritan theologian John Owen calls "gospel holiness."[4]

Gospel holiness is the correct understanding of sanctification. Self-improvement, a strong will, and diligence cannot and will not lead to sanctification. The process of being made holy is a radical, inward transformation flowing from our union with Christ. God's gracious gift of sanctification should be permeating the whole person—our thoughts, desires, and actions. *This is gospel holiness.*

All three persons of the Godhead are involved in our sanctification, just as they are in our justification. Jesus prays to God the Father, "Sanctify them in the truth; your word is truth" (John 17:17). Paul reminds the believers at Corinth, "You were washed, you were sanctified, you were justified in the name of the Lord Jesus Christ and by the Spirit of our God" (1 Corinthians 6:11). The Father, the Son, and the Spirit are all involved in making believers holy.[5]

Justification and sanctification are distinct but inseparable gifts of grace. The gospel channels God's grace both to accredit righteousness to us (our justification) and to grant the Spirit-wrought ability for us to live righteously (our sanctification). Justification is the act of God in which believers are *declared* righteous; sanctification is the act of God in which believers are *being made* righteous.

Unfortunately, sanctification is given less priority and sometimes treated like a nonessential or even optional aspect of the gospel—reserved only for spiritually mature Christians.[6] Such misunderstanding has resulted in many who call themselves Christians who are nowhere on the path of sanctification. They believe faith in Christ is somehow compatible with sinful desires of the flesh—for example, flirting and fantasizing with romantic passions that have no proper, godly end. Straddling the fence has no place in sanctification.

This serious deception stems from a failure to realize the depth of our depravity. As we saw earlier concerning the doctrine of sin, the extent of the fall of Adam and Eve is twofold: (1) we're guilty and in need of forgiveness, and (2) our moral condition has been polluted and corrupted.

When we ask an average churchgoer about salvation, the response mostly focuses on the forgiveness of our sins. Through faith, the Christian is indeed forgiven. However, this resolves only the first catastrophe of the Fall—our guilt. The second remains—our sin nature. Sanctification is God's provision to rectify our corrupted nature that seeks out and takes pleasure in sin.[7]

The process of becoming holy is essential and necessary in the life of the individual who has been saved by grace through faith in Christ. Our righteousness is bound up in Christ's righteousness, which is why imperfect believers can still be called "saints" (Romans 1:7; 2 Corinthians 1:1). Our Savior's death and resurrection have perfected for all time those he came to save. We stand holy before God, and through human action this can be neither improved nor lost.

Sanctification is evidence of true faith and results in both repentance and mortification of sin. This doesn't mean we experience perfect sinlessness or an absence of temptations in our daily lives. To better understand sanctification, we must recognize it has three aspects in light of God's grand story: positional (past), progressive (present), and perfected (future). We *have* been sanctified; we *are* being sanctified; and we *will* be sanctified.

Positional Sanctification

"We have been sanctified through the offering of the body of Jesus Christ once for all" (Hebrews 10:10). At the moment of conversion, positional sanctification is an instantaneous act of God's grace. It is definitive and once for all because Christ *is* our sanctification and we're united with him in his death and resurrection (1 Corinthians 1:30; Romans 6:5).

Positional sanctification means an actual break from the power of sin; we are "dead to sin" (Romans 6:11). It also means actual newness of life; we're "a new creation. The old has passed away; behold, the new has come" (2 Corinthians 5:17). Holiness is based solely on Christ's perfection, not ours.

Progressive Sanctification

"For by a single offering he has perfected for all time those who are being sanctified" (Hebrews 10:14). Sanctification is also progressive because, in this life, no one is without sin (1 John 1:8). The daily process of struggle and growth is a work of God in and through us, making us more and more like Christ. The gradual work of the Holy Spirit produces tangible evidence of our union with Christ in his death and resurrection.

God's grace enables those who are saved to "put on the Lord Jesus Christ, and make no provision for the flesh, to gratify its desires" (Romans 13:14). Paul also explains that sanctification is something we are still attaining: "Now that you have been set free from sin and have become slaves of God, the fruit you get leads to sanctification and its end, eternal life" (Romans 6:22). Sanctification in light of union with Christ means that we can live holy lives because with him we have already died and been raised in holiness.[8]

Perfect Sanctification

"Now may the God of peace himself sanctify you completely, and may your whole spirit and soul and body be kept blameless at the coming of our Lord Jesus Christ" (1 Thessalonians 5:23). Sanctification is brought to completion when we are fully united with Christ in the consummation. It will be at this point that positional sanctification becomes wholly realized.

This future aspect of sanctification speaks to the believer's perfected state in glory. When Christ returns, all things will be made new (Revelation 21:5), and "we shall be like him, because we shall see him as he is" (1 John 3:2). Thus, sanctification is positional, progressive, and perfect.

Paul explains that when one turns to the Lord, the journey of progressive sanctification begins: "We all, with unveiled face, beholding the glory of the Lord, are being transformed into the same image from one degree of glory to another" (2 Corinthians 3:18). Notice that we're being transformed into "the same image." That image is the Lord Jesus Christ. Paul tells us in Colossians 1:15 that the Son himself "is the image of the invisible God, the firstborn of all creation."

Michelangelo envisioned an image of his final product and understood the process it would take to get there. Likewise, our end is Jesus Christ, and the process is the gift of sanctification. God makes us righteous and conforms us to the image of Christ through our union with him. Sanctification is rooted not in our achievements but in the work of God in Christ through the Spirit.

The truth that Jesus Christ himself is our sanctification clears up some misunderstandings. We've already dispelled the myth that temptation is somehow incompatible with sanctification and the Christian life. If Jesus was tempted, then it should be no surprise that his followers will also be tempted.

Take note of these words of warning from Jesus himself: "Temptations to sin are sure to come" (Luke 17:1). It's not a matter of *if* we're tempted but *when* (1 Corinthians 10:13). It's therefore no shock that a sanctified Christian *might* still experience same-sex temptations.

This much I know is true: I have been changed—I'm a new creature in Christ—and that change is vital and real. I have a new heart, and my mind is renewed. Before conversion, I was indifferent toward Christ, which is equivalent to hatred. Now I love Christ, I want to please the Father, and I desire his holiness. This is real change even with the reality of my sin nature and in the midst of ongoing temptations.

God has redeemed us, and he has transformed us—and as such, we have new loyalties. These new loyalties and priorities grow deeper and stronger as we mature in Christ. Christ fights our battles now—even battles with indwelling sin. As I said before, because of our union with Christ, we can hate our sin without hating ourselves.

God *has* changed me.

BAD FRUIT ON VINES

The Good Fruit of Sanctification

As a kid, I was fascinated by Greek mythology. While it was never taught in the public schools I attended, I found it in the library and read it on my own. I could tell you all the different Greek gods and demigods, their stories, and even names from the corresponding Roman pantheon. To me, this was an intriguing world of ancient superheroes and villains. Homer's *Odyssey* describes one interesting group of antagonists, the Sirens.

Sirens were dangerous female creatures who sang away the minds of those sailing by. The sweetness of their song led to sure shipwreck on the rocky coast. Around these beasts lay a great heap of rotting flesh and bones from their bewitched prey. In this epic poem, Homer narrates that Odysseus was the first mortal to survive the Sirens' enchanting melodies. He ordered his men to tie him to the ship's mast while their own ears were plugged with wax as they sailed past.

It's usually understood that the seduction of the Sirens' song had a sexual and erotic tone to it. But note their words to Odysseus as he passed them:

Sea rovers here take joy
  Voyaging onward,

As from our song of Troy
Greybeard and rower-boy
Goeth more learnèd.[1]

The Sirens promised not only joy and pleasure for the journey but also wisdom and knowledge to old and young. Duplicity at its worst is the kind that leads to death. God's Word warns us to take heed how we hear. In 1 Thessalonians 5:21–22, Paul instructs that discernment is the responsibility of every believer: "Test everything; hold fast what is good. Abstain from every form of evil."

The apostle John also warns of the prevalence of false teaching: "Beloved, do not believe every spirit, but test the spirits to see whether they are from God, for many false prophets have gone out into the world" (1 John 4:1). Jesus reserves one of the most damning indictments for those who deceive: "Whoever causes one of these little ones who believe in me to sin, it would be better for him to have a great millstone fastened around his neck and to be drowned in the depth of the sea" (Matthew 18:6; see Mark 9:42; Luke 17:1–2).

Gay activist Matthew Vines begins his book *God and the Gay Christian* by asserting that the church's rejection of same-sex relationships is "harmful to the long-term well-being of most gay people" and that for some this rejection "fuels despair to the point of suicide."[2] For Vines, the teaching that same-sex desire and behavior are sinful produces "bad fruit." He tries to substantiate this bold claim with the words of Jesus:

Beware of false prophets, who come to you in sheep's clothing but
inwardly are ravenous wolves. You will recognize them by their
fruits. Are grapes gathered from thornbushes, or figs from thistles?
So, every healthy tree bears good fruit, but the diseased tree bears

bad fruit. A healthy tree cannot bear bad fruit, nor can a diseased tree bear good fruit. Every tree that does not bear good fruit is cut down and thrown into the fire. Thus you will recognize them by their fruits. (Matthew 7:15–20)

Vines concludes, "If something bears bad fruit, it cannot be a good tree. And if something bears good fruit, it cannot be a bad tree."[3] In Vines's line of thought, church doctrines and teachings are essentially measured by whether they produce "good fruit" or "bad fruit."

Matthew is a bright young man who attended Harvard for three semesters and never received a bachelor's degree. His problematic hermeneutics is on display from the start—an unsettling foretaste of the rest of the book. No matter how hard Vines tries, Jesus's use of "bad fruit" quite plainly cannot mean physical harm or emotional despair.

To conclude that "bad fruit" refers to suicide, attempted suicide, or even suicidal ideation requires a biblical interpreter to abandon basic exegetical principles. Furthermore, for Vines, hardship and distress are utterly incompatible with his idea of the Christian life. Matthew's irresponsible methodology is essentially a dance with deception.

This is a dismissal of the core doctrines of sanctification, repentance, and suffering. But the road to holiness and the path of repentance is paved with suffering. These truths are hard bought through Christ's perfect work on the cross. Regrettably, the church in America has an anemic theology of suffering—which explains how easily false teachers creep in among the sheep as ravenous wolves, tickling the ears with messages of ease and comfort!

Vines's interpretation leaves no room for suffering and cross bearing in the life of the believer. Those who think it's too hard to resist same-sex desires credulously believe that the Christian life must be struggle-free.

Matthew Vines simply represents a new iteration of the health, wealth, and prosperity movement. But the reality is that there's no gospel without suffering and pain.

Mortification of sin is not easy and will undoubtedly bring some distress. Jesus says,

> If your right eye causes you to sin, tear it out and throw it away.
> For it is better that you lose one of your members than that your
> whole body be thrown into hell. And if your right hand causes
> you to sin, cut it off and throw it away. For it is better that you
> lose one of your members than that your whole body go into
> hell. (Matthew 5:29–30)

Yet Vines would consider tearing out and throwing away as "bad fruit." This is the reality: sanctification is death. It involves a radical amputation of sin in our lives. The process is neither comfortable nor painless. "If anyone would come after me, let him deny himself and take up his cross daily and follow me. For whoever would save his life will lose it, but whoever loses his life for my sake will save it" (Luke 9:23–24; Luke 17:33).

Many Christians want to follow Jesus, but they're unwilling to deny themselves and take up their cross daily. Denying ourselves means denying everything for the sake of Christ—even our sexuality. In addition, taking up our cross doesn't mean bearing a difficult burden or struggle, as many take it. The cross in the Greco-Roman world never meant a burden. It signified death—one of the most gruesome and painful forms of death known to humankind. Jesus is telling you to pick that up.

We have so sanitized what it means to follow Jesus. We want Instagram Jesus—a nice me-centered app that is really not about following

Jesus but about following my friends and getting more to follow me. Following Jesus should cost us everything; if it doesn't, we're following the wrong Jesus.

Vines accuses us of spreading false teaching by encouraging same-sex-attracted individuals to endure a difficult life of singleness—bad fruit. Or it is Vines who is spreading false teaching by inducing others to affirm, celebrate, and live in unrepentant sin—bad fruit. Which is it? Both can't be true.

Jesus's words about causing his "little ones" to sin—bear bad fruit—are far too sobering to make this a trivial matter. Eternity is at stake here, not merely physical harm or well-being.

Excursus: Suicide Ideation

Before we discuss the hermeneutical improbability of Vines's interpretation, I want to say a few things about suicide. The higher incidence of suicide among youth identifying as gay has been documented—for all youth, not just those in Christian homes.[4]

Our response should be grave concern, deep compassion, and vigilant action. To our shame, evangelical Christians have often ignored this or brushed it off—even with an attitude that such deaths are somehow deserved. Such a glib response does not reflect the gospel truth that everyone is created in God's image and in need of his saving grace.

On the other side, many gay activists assert in error that these suicides are *because* the church continues to reject same-sex relationships. Author Jen Hatmaker and her husband are examples of those who blame gay youth suicides on the church's position against same-sex relationships.[5]

It's true that studies have found an association between parental rejection and a higher risk of suicide ideation among youth who identify as gay.[6] However, these studies do not in any way delve into whether those parents believe same-sex relationships are sinful or, more importantly, whether those parents are even Christian.

In addition, secular researchers have noted a study in the Netherlands revealing that "even in a country with a comparatively tolerant climate regarding homosexuality, homosexual men were at much higher risk for suicidality than heterosexual men."[7] The Netherlands was the first country in the world to legalize same-sex marriage in 2001, and many consider it the most gay-affirming country in the world.

In 2015, a European Union survey showed that 91 percent of those surveyed in the Netherlands believed same-sex marriage should be allowed throughout Europe—the highest percentage of any EU member country.[8] If the church's rejection of same-sex relationships causes suicides, then the Netherlands—where the evangelical church has a minimal presence—should have considerably fewer suicides. This unambiguously is not the case.

Currently there's no scientific evidence that the biblical stance on sexuality actually causes suicidality among gays. We just don't yet know. Jumping to the wrong conclusion distracts from discovering the real problem. In actuality, the blood may not be on the hands of evangelical Christians holding to biblical sexuality. Rather, the real, lasting, and eternal harm may be elsewhere—specifically leading Jesus's weaker "little ones" into sin.

Bad Fruit

Let's get back to the illegitimacy of "bad fruit" being physical or emotional harm. The gospel of Matthew contains more instances of the Greek word *karpos* or "fruit" than any other New Testament book—nineteen occurrences. Prior to Matthew 7:15–20, "fruit" appears in Matthew 3:7–10 when John the Baptist rebukes the Pharisees:

> You brood of vipers! Who warned you to flee from the wrath to come? Bear fruit in keeping with repentance. And do not presume to say to yourselves, "We have Abraham as our father," for I tell you, God is able from these stones to raise up children for Abraham. Even now the axe is laid to the root of the trees. Every tree therefore that does not bear good fruit is cut down and thrown into the fire.

Notice closely that last sentence: "Every tree therefore that does not bear good fruit is cut down and thrown into the fire." Except for the adverb *therefore,* this statement is identical to what Jesus says in Matthew 7:19: "Every tree that does not bear good fruit is cut down and thrown into the fire." This is no coincidence, nor was the similarity unintentional. The two Matthean passages are intimately connected; good fruit is essentially repentance, and bad fruit is unrepentance. This is consistent with Jesus's words in Luke 13:

> There were some present at that very time who told him about the Galileans whose blood Pilate had mingled with their sacrifices. And he answered them, "Do you think that these Galileans were worse sinners than all the other Galileans, because they suffered in this way? No, I tell you; but unless you repent, you will all likewise perish. Or those eighteen on whom the tower in Siloam fell and killed them: do you think that they were worse offenders than all the others who lived in Jerusalem? No, I tell you; but unless you repent, you will all likewise perish."

And he told this parable: "A man had a fig tree planted in his vineyard, and he came seeking fruit on it and found none. And he said to the vinedresser, 'Look, for three years now I have come seeking fruit on this fig tree, and I find none. Cut it down. Why should it use up the ground?' And he answered him, 'Sir, let it alone this year also, until I dig around it and put on manure. Then if it should bear fruit next year, well and good; but if not, you can cut it down.'" (verses 1–9)

Studying "bad fruit" in Greek makes it even clearer. The word "bad" can be expressed in different ways. One is *kakos,* meaning "bad or harmful." Another is *poneros,* which has a moral connotation of "wickedness or evil." In the gospel of Matthew, *poneros* occurs twenty-six times, and all these usages have a connotation of wickedness or evil.

In Matthew 7, Jesus uses *poneros* for "bad fruit," not *kakos.* So "bad fruit" should really be "wicked fruit" or "evil fruit." In spite of Vines's assertion, "bad fruit" does *not* symbolize a harmful, painful, or inherently unpleasant experience; it's simply something that is morally wicked—unrepentance. Studying the context and the Greek, it's not possible for "bad fruit" to mean depression or suicide.

In addition, Jesus is not referring to *something* bearing bad fruit—such as false teaching, which according to Vines is biblical sexuality. Rather, Jesus is referring to *someone* bearing bad fruit—namely, a false prophet. Unfortunately, false prophets back then looked and acted like Christians and were no easier to spot than they are today. "Beware of false prophets, who come to you in sheep's clothing but inwardly are ravenous wolves" (Matthew 7:15).

False teachers winsomely and convincingly claim to know the will of God but really do not. What makes them so dangerous is their broad influence and sweet-sounding distortions of God's truth—which aren't immediately apparent. Even worse, false teachers have the outward "trappings of piety and righteousness—the obvious marks of being part of the people of God."[9]

What's even more ironic is that Vines completely misses or ignores Jesus's unambiguous warning in the verses right before the good fruit and bad fruit passage in Matthew 7:15–20. "Enter by the narrow gate. For the gate is wide and the way is easy that leads to destruction, and those who enter by it are many. For the gate is narrow and the way is hard that leads to life, and those who find it are few" (Matthew 7:13–14). Irrespective of Vines's implausible interpretation, the narrow gate is *hard*—but it leads to life.

So does biblical sexuality actually lead to harm? Or does this false teaching on bad fruit lead to long-term harm? I'll let you be the judge. Matthew Vines's Reformation Project, promoting full inclusion of LGBTQ people by reforming church teaching, is founded on this faulty concept of "bad fruit." If a leader blatantly takes Scripture out of context like this, twisting the Bible to say what it doesn't say, everything else he teaches should be suspect.

Let's read our Lord's forceful and compelling admonition again: "Whoever causes one of these little ones who believe in me to sin, it would be better for him to have a great millstone fastened around his neck and to be drowned in the depth of the sea" (Matthew 18:6).

My prayer is that those who have ears to hear will hear. And for those who do not, I pray they will accept God's gracious and loving gift of repentance. Repentance is good fruit. And using Jesus's words, rejecting repentance is truly bad fruit.

17

COMPASSION

The Only Way Forward

I'll never forget that smell of urine. It was 1996, a few years before I became a Christian. The dilapidated Cook County Hospital was more like a haunted house than a place of healing. My good friend Jordan had fallen sick, and this was the only reason I was in that awful place.

Jordan was a well-known entertainer in the gay community, but few knew he was HIV positive. While performing at a couple of Chicago gay clubs, he got really sick and came down with pneumonia. For someone with a compromised immune system, this was life threatening.

I took a few days off from dental school and drove up from Louisville to see him. When I arrived, I was told he was quarantined in the intensive care unit, so I had to put on a mask, gown, and gloves. When I saw him lying in the bed, what shocked me most wasn't that my friend—normally young and strong—looked tired and emaciated; it was that he was completely alone. None of his thousands of fans or friends had come to visit him. I couldn't help but think, *Is this how it's going to end for me too?*

I stayed the night with Jordan in the dark, dreary hospital room, and in the morning, for some crazy reason, I felt compelled to call home. I knew where my Christian parents stood when it came to homosexuality, but I just wanted to hear a familiar voice. When I called, my mother was so excited that she offered to drive down to see me and my friend. I was a bit shocked; I never expected she would want to meet any of my gay friends.

Before long, my parents were down the hall from his room getting gowned up. I was so worried they might say something that would offend Jordan, especially in his vulnerable state. But my fear went away when I saw my mother's eyes peeping over her mask, full of grace and compassion. She gave me a big hug—then went over and hugged Jordan as well. We sat there in the room for more than half an hour, chatting and laughing. My parents brought up no sensitive topics. Instead, we just talked like old friends.

Their compassion took me by surprise. It had been a while since I'd seen them, and after they'd become Christians, I expected them to be judgmental toward Jordan. But as we sat in that dank and gloomy hospital room, the only people with me at the bedside of this famous performer, showing compassion in his time of need, were strangers—my Christian parents.

My father and mother loved me and my friend Jordan that day. The narrative is often told of Christian parents rejecting their gay children and being unloving and of unbelieving parents really loving and supporting their gay sons and daughters. However, I experienced the exact opposite. Before my parents came to Christ, they rejected me; only *after* their conversion did they love their gay son and show compassion to a stranger.

Who Is My Neighbor?

We discussed in several of the first chapters the truth about who we are. Then we established biblical sexuality in the next several chapters. Afterward, we illustrated the beautiful theology of marriage and singleness. In the last couple of chapters, we discussed sanctification, suffering, and repentance. Now we turn to the practical—showing compassion and love.

First, how do we love strangers? It begins with good theology—namely, that "all have sinned and fall short of the glory of God" (Romans 3:23). As a matter of fact, we can't even love as God intends until we fully grasp and accept for ourselves the reality of God's grand story—creation, fall, redemption, and consummation.

It starts by knowing that we're all created in God's image and that all the redeemed saints are still sinners saved and made holy by God's grace. Not until my parents were able to realize that *their* struggle with sin was not much different from *my* struggle with sin could they love and have compassion toward my gay friend Jordan.

A favorite parable of mine is the story of the good Samaritan—a quintessential example of exhibiting compassion to a neighbor in need. I've read that parable many times, but in my previous readings, I always missed a key detail found in Jesus's final question to the lawyer.

His question at the end of the parable completely alters the crux and tenor of this narrative that I thought I knew so well. Jesus's parables aren't meant to make us comfortable or feel good. They're meant to provoke us out of our comfort zone and make us consider, *What still needs to be changed in my life?*

The parable is precipitated by a simple question in Luke 10:25. An expert of Mosaic law tries to test Jesus by asking him, "What shall I do to inherit eternal life?" Jesus instead tests the tester: "What is written in the Law? How do you read it?" (verse 26). Probably having heard Jesus previously, the lawyer responds by mentioning the two greatest commandments: love God and love your neighbor.

The lawyer then pounces with this question: "Who is my neighbor?" (verse 29). Revealing his true motive to justify his lack of compassion, the lawyer really wants to know who is *not* his neighbor. Here is Jesus's response:

A man was going down from Jerusalem to Jericho, and he fell
among robbers, who stripped him and beat him and departed,
leaving him half dead. Now by chance a priest was going down
that road, and when he saw him he passed by on the other side.
So likewise a Levite, when he came to the place and saw him,
passed by on the other side. But a Samaritan, as he journeyed,
came to where he was, and when he saw him, he had compassion. He went to him and bound up his wounds, pouring on oil
and wine. Then he set him on his own animal and brought him
to an inn and took care of him. And the next day he took out
two denarii and gave them to the innkeeper, saying, "Take care
of him, and whatever more you spend, I will repay you when I
come back." (verses 30–35)

First, let's recall what prompted this parable: the lawyer's question,
"Who is my neighbor?" From the story, it seems quite simple. The good
Samaritan sees the traveler who fell among the robbers as his neighbor.
Therefore, anyone in need is our neighbor. However, this is the key detail
I had previously missed in Jesus's final question. If Jesus meant for the
traveler to be the neighbor, then we'd expect Jesus to ask, "Which of these
three, do you think, treated the man who fell among the robbers as his
neighbor?"

However, this is *not* what Jesus asks.

Instead, in verse 36, Jesus asks, "Which of these three, do you think,
proved to be a neighbor to the man who fell among the robbers?" Ob-
serve the difference. Jesus is a master storyteller, and as he often does, he
turns the scenario on its head with a provocative twist. In a massive rever-
sal of roles, the neighbor isn't the traveler who fell among the robbers; the
neighbor is the Samaritan.

The parable has a profound thrust, particularly in light of the fact that Jews regarded Samaritans among the least respected people—eating with them was equivalent to eating pork.[1] Yet the parable's significance is much more than simply transcending our human-made boundaries of race or social status to love our neighbor.

Jesus knows it is next to impossible for this Jewish lawyer to go against his human nature to love the unlovable Samaritan unless something radical happens in his life. The key is found within the story, particularly the point of view from which this tale is told—not from the perspective of the good Samaritan but from the perspective of the traveler who fell among the robbers.[2]

The only way for the Jewish lawyer to love a Samaritan as his neighbor is to relive this parable from that traveler's point of view. More than likely, the man who fell among the robbers was Jewish himself and therefore hated Samaritans. One day on his way to Jericho, he's jumped by a gang of thugs and knocked unconscious. The last thing he remembers is his nose being crushed by punches to the face and the intense pain of his ribs cracking from kicks to the gut.

This is it . . . I'm going to die.

Now imagine him waking up confused, lying in a warm bed. A stranger who says he's an innkeeper quickly brings him food and drink, then tends to his wounds. Still in excruciating pain, the man who fell among the robbers is shocked just to be alive. Assuming it was this innkeeper who saved his life, the traveler begins to thank him. But what comes out of the innkeeper's mouth changes his life forever.

The innkeeper tells him that it was a Samaritan who stopped, had compassion, bound the man's wounds, and brought him to this inn. This Samaritan promised to pay the full amount necessary for the traveler to be fully healed.

Let that sink in for a moment. You tell me: Would the man who fell among the robbers be changed when he heard this news? Would this traveler—a Jew who despised Samaritans—now have a totally different perspective toward Samaritans or any other stranger for that matter?

With this in mind, let's answer the question again: *Who is my neighbor?* I bet if the lawyer really put himself in the shoes of the traveler, he would have a completely different perspective on life. Jesus isn't exhorting us simply to love people in need; he commands us to love people we perceive to be despised, undeserving, and foreign.

Jesus subtly and creatively communicates that the only way we can love our neighbor—the only way a Jew can love a despised Samaritan or a Christian can love a stranger—is to put ourselves in the shoes of the man who fell among the robbers. So let's do that.

I was going down from Jerusalem to Jericho, and *I* fell among robbers, who stripped *me* and beat *me* and departed, leaving *me* half dead. Now by chance a priest was going down that road, and when he saw *me* he passed by on the other side. So likewise a Levite, when he came to the place and saw *me,* passed by on the other side. But a Samaritan, as he journeyed, came to where *I* was, and when he saw *me,* he had compassion. He went to *me* and bound up *my* wounds, pouring on oil and wine. Then he set *me* on his own animal and brought *me* to an inn and took care of *me.* And the next day he took out two denarii and gave them to the innkeeper, saying, "Take care of *this individual,* and whatever more you spend, I will repay you when I come back."

If we're honest, what happened to this traveler isn't much different from what has happened to each one of us in the grand scheme of God's redemptive story. The consequence of the Fall has robbed us, beaten us, and left us dead at the side of the road. Everyone we might expect to help has instead passed us by. But one person stopped and had compassion.

That someone is Jesus.

Jesus even paid the ultimate price of his own life so we would be healed. Only when we find solidarity with the traveler who fell among the robbers, realizing Jesus is the good Samaritan showing compassion, are we truly able to love our neighbor as ourselves.

The main takeaway of this parable is not love your neighbor by trying hard to be like the good Samaritan but rather love your neighbor by realizing you are the traveler and Jesus, the good Samaritan, has loved you first.

How can the Samaritan represent both the despised and rejected individual whom we must love as our neighbor *and* Jesus who loved us first? The answer is found in both the Old Testament and the New Testament. In Isaiah 53:3, the Suffering Servant and coming Messiah is described: "He was despised and rejected by men."

In Matthew 25:35–36, Jesus explains that showing compassion for others is showing compassion to Jesus. "For I was hungry and you gave me food, I was thirsty and you gave me drink, I was a stranger and you welcomed me, I was naked and you clothed me, I was sick and you visited me, I was in prison and you came to me."

When my parents showed compassion to Jordan, a total stranger, they didn't do it by mustering up goodness from the depths of their own hearts. They did it because they realized they're sinners and just as broken as the man who fell among the robbers. They loved me and Jordan because Jesus loved them first. Their love was really an overflow of Christ's abundant love for them.

Understanding the parable in this way, we realize that loving our neighbor begins not by *being like* the good Samaritan but by *being* the man who fell among the robbers. In essence, to save others, we need to be saved first! When we recognize this, our love is not from the goodness within our own hearts, but it's really a reflection of the One who loved us first.

Hide or Go Seek

Showing compassion is a must, but how can we walk alongside those who hide and are afraid to open up about their struggles, particularly regarding sexuality?

While researching for my doctoral thesis, I investigated some of the reasons Christians with same-sex attractions didn't disclose their struggles, which sometimes resulted in them seeking help from the secular world.[3] We evangelicals feel free to open up about a multitude of difficulties—pornography addictions, eating disorders, alcoholism, sex abuse, and so on. But many feel that same-sex attraction is the one thing they cannot share with another Christian.

If the Christian church functioned as it should, this stigma would end. From my own experience, I know the best place to work through matters related to sexuality is in the body of Christ, where God's truth is our firm foundation and biblical sexuality is the unambiguous standard.

Instead, our youth often seek answers from the world since they expect to be judged by the church simply for experiencing same-sex attractions. They fear no one will understand them. It's no wonder many end up having an incorrect understanding of sexuality.

As part of my doctoral research, I surveyed those with same-sex attractions and asked open-ended questions about their experiences in the Christian community. Many of their responses broke my heart. One answered, "I was terrified that I would be judged and ostracized for something I didn't want and something that wasn't in my control."

Another said, "I didn't feel like I would be understood. . . . I thought that I would at least be rejected by peers and maybe even made fun of." Yet another gave this reason for his silence: "I was terrified to tell close friends for this reason: I couldn't bear to lose some of the most meaningful friendships in my life." Of all the responses from the eighty individuals in my study, these heart-rending responses were sadly the norm.

I've been teaching at Moody for over ten years, and every semester I've had students confide in me regarding their sexuality. They're often struggling alone, and because of their isolation, some battle depression and even thoughts of suicide. They're afraid that if they go to their Christian family members, to their pastor or youth pastor, they won't find mercy, grace, and understanding. Unfortunately, that's often true.

Our public schools and universities have designated safe spaces where people are supposed to be able to go and express their experiences freely without being ostracized. But I wonder, Shouldn't the safest place in the world be the church? Of course, the body of Christ shouldn't be satisfied merely with being safe. Our goal is to be safe *and* redemptive. But are we?

Some of you might be thinking of a particular close friend right now—someone you believe may have same-sex attractions. Can you bring it up? How should you ask? *Don't.* Even if we have a desire to walk through this with our friend, we must practice patience. Sexuality is a very personal and private matter.

We need to allow our friends to open up about their sexuality in their own time, not ours. But what you *can* do is give assurance of your friendship. Start with this: "I'm thankful God put you in my life. Whatever you say or do won't change our friendship." This creates a safe place and invites them in.

In my experience, Christians are sometimes surprised to discover that a friend or loved one experiences same-sex attractions. "I grew up with him," they say, baffled. "How could this have happened? We went to church and youth group together; his parents are Christians—he was even homeschooled!" But how is it possible we don't understand that *everybody* is tempted with sin? Does being raised in a Christian home and attending church as a child make us exempt from struggling with our flesh? Of course not!

If we're redeemed followers of Christ, we should be open and honest about the fact that we don't have it all together. We'll be a safe and redemptive place for all our brothers and sisters to admit together, "I'm broken, and I desperately need Jesus." Even though our individual struggles on the particular level may look a little different, the overall problem is the same: sin. And the overall answer is the same: new life and daily renewal in Christ.

As brothers and sisters in Christ, we need to come together as a loving and intimate spiritual family and walk hand in hand with those who are struggling—not so that we can fix them, not because we have all the answers, but because we know someone who does. And his name is Jesus.

OUTREACH

Guidelines for Our Conversations

Several of my Moody classmates are missionaries sharing the love of Christ and the beauty of the gospel with Muslims in closed countries. Sharing the gospel in the Middle East requires a lot of creativity and patience. Without rushing into theological differences, we must first be sensitive and respectful, particularly in light of their negative perception of Christians.

Unfortunately, many Muslims perceive that Christians have deep animosity toward them. Although I personally don't know any born-again believers who hate Muslims, perception is reality. In light of this, we begin by patiently building relationships, and we don't rush to point out how they're wrong or living in sin. Avoid an us-versus-them attitude. If our hope is to lead Muslims to Christ, we must establish trust before we broach controversial topics.

I've always thought we should model how we minister to gays and lesbians after how we minister to Muslims. At the surface level, the two groups are very different. However, both share something in common— how they perceive Christians. Like Muslims, the perception of many gays and lesbians is that we have deep animosity toward them.

Therefore, ministry to the gay community also requires a lot of creativity and patience. Without rushing into theological differences, we must be sensitive and respectful. With our gay friends, we begin by patiently building relationships, and we don't rush to point out how they're wrong or living in sin. If our hope is to lead our gay friends to Christ, we must establish trust before we broach controversial topics.

We must *live* the gospel before we *preach* the gospel. Actually, the gay community may be one of the most unreached people groups of our day. How do we share the love of Christ and the beauty of the gospel with our loved ones and friends in the gay community who don't know Christ? What follows are a few dos and don'ts.

Things to Avoid

Ignorance is *not* bliss. What we don't know *can* hurt us—or at least substantially hinder our ability to share Christ with someone we love. Without realizing it, we can easily offend someone by something we do and crush our chances to share Christ. So here are some things to avoid.

Don't Compare Same-Sex Relationships with Other Sins

With your atheist gay friends, it's not helpful to compare their sin with other sins like jealousy, pride, or gossip. You might use this with other unbelievers because everyone has been guilty of these seemingly minor sins. But the problem is that your gay friends do not believe their same-sex relationships are sinful.

In addition, when we say that "homosexuality is sin," because our gay friends believe "being gay" is who they are, they hear us saying that the core of their being—their entire person—is sinful. Starting with the wrong identity leads to a misunderstanding of the doctrine of sin.

I believe it's much more productive to talk about identity. "Who are you? Tell me more about you." That's a great place to start with anyone. And press into what they mean by *gay* and whether attractions should really be the core of who we are. This way, you'll be able to deepen the conversation and probably have a chance to share about your own identity in Christ. Share first about Jesus, not about morality.

Don't Use the Words Lifestyle *or* Choice

These two terms may fit well into our understanding of humanity and sin, for sinful behavior is an actual choice and continuing to sin is a way of life. However, those who don't have a Christian worldview can't separate their behaviors from who they are.

It can even be offensive to say to your gay friend that she "struggles" with same-sex attractions. When I lived as a gay man, this was not my "struggle," my "lifestyle," or my "choice." It was simply *who I was.* Again, the implications of a false identity are broad.

It's quite possible that your loved one or friend is overly sensitive and an unintentional use of a word could greatly offend him. If you're uncertain about what word or label to use, be honest and ask. Usually language is very important to our gay friends.

Just as missionaries need to learn new vocabulary, we need to learn the vocabulary of our gay friends. In the twenty years since I lived in the gay community, language has changed dramatically and I am learning the new terminology. I'm willing to meet people where they are by not using certain words and by speaking their language for the sake of pointing them to Christ.

Don't Say "Love the Sinner; Hate the Sin"—Just Do It

We love the saying "Love the sinner; hate the sin," but what we don't realize is that non-Christians hate it. When you tell your gay friends "I love you, but I hate your sin," they really don't feel loved! All they hear is what comes after "but." Do it; don't say it.

Actually, we must be very careful with how we use the conjunction *but*. For example, many Christian parents who receive news that their son or daughter is gay may say, "I love you, but . . ." When we say "but," it cancels everything that was just said. Instead, simply say "I love you" and save the rest for another day.

Don't Debate All the Time

While we're compelled to speak truth in love, we must also realize that people aren't debated into the kingdom. For example, when the Pharisees or Sadducees try to pull Jesus into a debate, he never falls into their trap. Sometimes he provides an answer to a much more important question, like whether they should pay taxes to Caesar (Matthew 22:15–22; Mark 12:13–17; Luke 20:20–26).

If we look carefully, we notice that Jesus tailors his responses. Before the chief priests, elders, Pilate, and Herod, Jesus sometimes simply doesn't answer (Matthew 27:12–14; Mark 15:5; Luke 23:9). To the crowds, whose hearts were dull, he speaks in parables (Matthew 13:10–15, 34–35). To the disciples, who were given ears to hear, Jesus explains the secrets of the kingdom of heaven (Matthew 13:11, 16).

There is a time for truth, and we just need to know the right time and the right manner to give it. Because Jesus *is* truth, there really was no need for him to defend himself. Sometimes the Son of God answers a question with a question. For example, in John 18:33–34, Pilate asks Jesus whether he was the king of the Jews. Jesus answers, "Do you say this of your own accord, or did others say it to you about me?"

Jesus turns the tables, and the questioner becomes the questioned. This causes the two to go deeper, beyond simply answering a yes or no question. What matters most is this: Will Pilate follow Jesus? In the same way, the most important thing is not that we convince others that same-sex relationships are sinful. Rather, the most important thing is whether people will receive the gift of faith and follow Jesus.

When an unbeliever asks us, "Is being gay a sin?" we can cause the conversation to go deeper by asking one of two questions: "How do you define sin?" or "What does it mean to be gay?" This will lead to a broader discussion about morality or identity.

If someone asks, "Do you think gays are going to hell?" I'd ask this: "What's your understanding of who deserves God's judgment?" Then you can have a great conversation about the character of God and the sinfulness of humanity. And this can easily segue into the necessity of Jesus as the perfect sacrifice for sin.

Knowing how to reply with good questions is probably one of the most effective forms of evangelism and apologetics.

Sharing Christ

You may have a gay son or daughter who has rejected the faith. How can you best share the light of Christ? Obviously, we must be sensitive to the leading of the Holy Spirit. Below is not a formula but just a few suggestions. Always remember that the main concern is not your son or daughter's sexuality or same-sex relationship. The larger issue is your son or daughter's heart. As I said earlier, my biggest sin wasn't same-sex sexual behavior; my biggest sin was unbelief.

Pray and Fast

To begin with prayer is a way to remind ourselves that only God changes hearts. As much as we love someone and as hard as we may try, we can't make someone believe in Jesus. When things seemed hopeless, my mother committed to focus not on hopelessness but on the promises of God. She recruited over a hundred prayer warriors from church and from her Bible Study Fellowship group, and together they cried out to God for me.

My mother began to pray a bold prayer: "Lord, do whatever it takes to bring this prodigal son to you." In her desperation, she fasted every Monday for eight years and once fasted thirty-nine days for me. She spent hours every morning in her prayer closet, reading her Bible and interceding for me and many others. She actually wrote out some of her prayers, and this is one of them:

> I'll stand in the gap for Christopher. I'll stand until the victory
> is won, until Christopher's heart changes. I'll stand in the gap
> every day, and there I will fervently pray. And Lord, just one
> favor: don't let me waver. If things get quite rough, which they
> may, I'll never give up on that son nor will You. Though the
> enemy seeks to destroy, I'll not quit as I intercede, though it
> may take years. I give you my fears and tears as I trust every
> moment I plead.

She prayed those prayers for eight years, and it seemed God wasn't answering them. But God did answer her prayers, just not in the way she expected. God's answer was, *Wait. Be still, and know that I am God.* (Psalm 46:10). During those difficult years, I wasn't changing and things were even getting worse for me. But what God intended for that time was that my parents would be changed, that they would be transformed, and that they would be trophies of God's mercy.

Oswald Chambers says, "We are not here to prove God answers prayer; we are here to be living monuments of God's grace."[1] As they lived out those years of waiting, my parents learned to walk and live as monuments of his grace as God drew them to himself each day.

Unfortunately, it seems like the church here in America has forgotten the spiritual discipline of fasting, relegating it to something only *super* Christians do. Just as giving and praying are not optional, fasting is expected of the believer—Jesus says not "if" but "when you fast" (Matthew 6:16–18). Fasting is a physical battle with our flesh that reminds us of the spiritual battle with our sin nature.

You may be familiar with *War Room,* the 2015 film about the power of prayer, written and produced by Alex and Stephen Kendrick. Author and Moody radio host Chris Fabry worked with the Kendrick brothers to adapt the film into a book, and it was released around the same time as the film. My parents and I received an early copy of the book and noticed on the dedication page that Fabry had written, "To Angela Yuan, prayer warrior."[2]

Many of us pray for our loved ones and friends, and we must continue to do so with persistence and anticipation. But how many in the gay community have not a single Christian praying for them? I wonder what would happen if the church committed to pray for the gay community, specifically for those we know who are gay. Wouldn't it be amazing if a revival broke out?

Listen

I don't remember where I heard this proverbial saying: "God gave us two ears and one mouth to remind us we should listen more than we speak." If we want our unbelieving gay friends to listen to us, we must first listen to them.

As you listen to your gay friends' stories about their partners, how might you respond? "I'm so happy for you" wouldn't be right. Instead, you can simply acknowledge his experience, saying, "I see that this person means a lot to you." Remember, acknowledging someone's feelings doesn't mean agreeing with her actions. The apostle Paul reminds us that "God's kindness is meant to lead you to repentance" (Romans 2:4).

Be Intentional

Don't be afraid to go across the street and invite your gay neighbors over for dinner. Some Christians fear that doing so condones their sin. But last time I checked, we usually have sinners over for dinner! We're only eating with them, not sinning with them. The self-righteous and hypocritical Pharisees spoke pejoratively about Jesus eating with tax collectors and sinners (Matthew 9:11; Mark 2:16). How can people know Christ if they never experience the love of Christ?

Similarly, some parents wonder whether having a child's partner in their home communicates approval. Parents, you must realize that your children don't doubt your position on homosexuality; they are uncertain whether you fully love them. You may object that you haven't done anything to imply that you don't love them. I believe you! But you must know that the world and their friends keep telling them that you do *not* really love them and that you don't really understand or know them—all because you are a Christian and think they're living in sin. Loving them is often like trying to push back against a tidal wave of distrust and skepticism.

How do you do this? By showering your kids with love. By clearly and repeatedly saying you love them. When I was off in a far country, my mother sent me Christian cards every other day. She signed every card, "Love you forever, Mom."

I didn't read them but tossed them in the trash. Yet she was planting seeds, and I certainly remember the cards now. Imagine if you sent your loved one a text twice every week this year. His heart would soften. It can be as simple as "Thinking about you today," "Hope you're having a blessed day," or "I love you, and I'm praying for you!"

I know some parents who did this, and their daughter told them, "Don't pray for me because I know what you're praying for!" I told them to respond, "I pray for everyone I love." How can a child argue with that? Also, our homes should always be open to our children and their friends. What a great opportunity to show what a Christian household looks like.

I know of parents who had a gay son. Initially they struggled with even meeting their son's partner. But after realizing that their son's partner also needed to know Christ, they began inviting him into their home. Some time passed, and the parents actually developed a strong relationship with their son's boyfriend. After several years, the two men actually split up, but the parents kept in touch with their son's ex. In an amazing turn of events, their son's ex-partner came to Christ, even expressing that the father was the only father figure he ever had in his life. You never really know the outcome of loving others in the name of Jesus!

Be Patient and Persistent

My parents prayed for eight years, and that's actually a relatively short period of time. I know people who've been praying for decades. If God was patient and persistent with us, shouldn't we be the same with others in their journey to God?

Standing in the gap can be long and tedious, but the example of Jesus as the Good Shepherd shows us that even one lost sheep is worth pursuing until found. We give up so easily because we have so little faith. As my mother prayed for me, she also prayed that God would give her perseverance. Like the persistent widow, my mother kept "bothering" God with her petition so he wouldn't forget (Luke 18:1–8).

I call it practicing the spiritual discipline of waiting. We always want things done in our own time. But often God simply wants us to trust him, and our job is to wait. And God then works on our child as we wait. However, this doesn't mean we do nothing, for we still pray and fast.

It's also about practicing the custom of presence—being available for our loved ones even when they don't want us. Then, when God works and does whatever it takes, our mere presence communicates that we are someone they can turn to.

Be Transparent

It's not easy to share the gospel with those whose hearts may be closed. If you pull out your Bible, they'll probably run or begin arguing with you. But there's something no one can take away from you, and that's what God has done in your own life.

If you're a follower of Christ, you shouldn't be the same as you were ten years ago, ten months ago, or even ten weeks ago! Be willing to talk about the amazing things God has done. New life in Christ should be more than something in your head. Living a gospel-centered life should be visible and tangible.

Personally, I would never have considered the gospel if I hadn't seen it lived out in my parents' lives. When I saw that Bible in the prison trash can, I wouldn't have picked it up if I hadn't seen the Bible lived out in my father's and mother's lives. I didn't leave pursuing a same-sex relationship because my parents convinced me it was sinful. I didn't leave it because they convinced me it was unhealthy. I left it because I was shown something better—and his name is Jesus.

The mandate we have to preach the gospel will be only empty words if our lives show no evidence of transformation. If Jesus Christ gives new life, it must show. If we have no joy in the midst of sorrow, hope in the midst of despair, peace in the midst of struggle, then actually we may need a revival in our own hearts first.

This is my point: we must show the beauty of the gospel lived out in our daily lives and let that be the foundation from which we proclaim the good news to the lost. No matter what people cling to, of all the fool's gold in the world—money, fame, career, power, happiness, or even a relationship—nothing comes close to the joy and satisfaction of a life fully surrendered to God.

Our job as followers of Christ is to live in a way that makes it unmistakable to a dying world that Jesus is better than anything this world has to offer.

RECEIVING THE NEWS

How to Respond When a Friend Opens Up

Many have a desire to minister to those who have same-sex attractions and those who identify as gay. This is good! We need to realize that our approach to those with same-sex attractions is not always going to be the same. If your gay friend does not know Christ, the focus must be outreach and evangelism. If your loved one with same-sex attractions is following Christ, the focus must be discipleship and mentoring.

But what about those who say they're Christian and think their same-sex relationship is *not* sinful? Let those who say such things never forget Jesus's sobering words—and let us all heed these words as well:

> Not everyone who says to me, "Lord, Lord," will enter the
> kingdom of heaven, but the one who does the will of my Father
> who is in heaven. On that day many will say to me, "Lord, Lord,
> did we not prophesy in your name, and cast out demons in your
> name, and do many mighty works in your name?" And then
> will I declare to them, "I never knew you; depart from me, you
> workers of lawlessness." (Matthew 7:21–23)

It's estimated that nearly three-quarters of Americans say they're Christian.[1] Wouldn't it be wonderful if this really were true? Regrettably, according to Jesus's words, not everyone who says he or she is a Christian is a Christian.

Although we cannot foresee people's eternal destinies (keep in mind that their journeys aren't over yet), we can consider today whether they are doing the Father's will or still working lawlessness. Are they bearing the good fruit of repentance or the bad fruit of unrepentance?

Thus, in light of all we've discussed, men and women who identify as gay and say, "I can have Jesus *and* my same-sex relationship," not only forsake biblical, gospel-centered sexuality but also distort the image of God and the doctrines of sin, identity, desire, singleness, sanctification, and gospel-suffering.

Actually, they're advocating a false, neoprosperity gospel. These individuals want to belong to Jesus without giving up their sexual identity. This anemic theology of suffering is Christ without the cross—which is no gospel at all. Until they're ready to surrender *all* and be crucified with Christ (Galatians 2:20), our aim with these individuals is to share the true gospel—that is, evangelism and outreach.

I already covered a few things on sharing Christ with gay loved ones who don't know Christ in the previous chapter. Those suggestions also apply to individuals who hold to this false gospel. They need to be born again. They need to deny themselves, pick up their cross, and follow Jesus!

Some well-intentioned organizations encourage a posture shift by simply showing compassion to the gay community—which is very important. However, if the end goal is simply love devoid of being born again, following Jesus, and pursuing sanctification and discipleship, we actually neuter the gospel.

Sometimes in our enthusiasm to love, we have no plan for those who do believe. Our outreach becomes an end in itself without discipleship and sanctification in mind. This is equivalent to abandoning a newborn baby to fend for itself. Just as an infant is dependent on others to grow, so is a new believer. If you're in a position to mentor your friend or loved one who has same-sex attractions, do it! However, if you're just a peer or good friend, encourage him or her to pursue a discipleship relationship with a godly mentor. Being a disciple and making disciples are indispensable aspects of following Jesus. Evangelism must support and be supported by discipleship.

I will discuss discipleship in the next chapter. But what if your Christian friend or loved one opens up to you about his or her same-sex attractions? What should you say? How should you respond?[2]

Don't Freak Out

This may go without saying, but I know people are often overwhelmed when receiving this news from a loved one. Parents wonder, *What did we do wrong? How did this happen?* Remember, we're all sinners and your loved one's sin struggle is just that: a sin struggle. If we understand the truth in Scripture about us, everyone struggles with sin. That's nothing new!

Because we all are tempted with sin, we all need the Holy Spirit to empower us to flee daily from illicit behavior and desire. As you're listening to your loved one, reflect Jesus, who is "full of grace and truth" (John 1:14). Don't forget that our Father is "merciful and gracious, slow to anger, and abounding in steadfast love and faithfulness" (Exodus 34:6). Do your best to love in this way.

Thank Your Friend

Opening up with a Christian friend about same-sex attractions can be one of the scariest things to do. Imagine keeping something inside for years, if not decades. It would produce layers upon layers, years upon years of stigma and shame. These individuals are often so afraid that if someone finds out, they will be judged, ostracized, and even rejected.

Most likely, it took months for your friends or loved ones to get to this day and confide in you. They probably rehearsed over and over in their minds what to tell you and how exactly to say it. Just the fact that your loved ones opened up to you speaks volumes about you—you're someone people can trust. Tell them how much you appreciate being invited to journey with them. Commit to walking with them through the highs and the lows.

Be a Friend, Not an Expert

You may feel ill equipped because you've never had attractions toward the same sex. So how in the world can you help your loved one or friend? I've heard this legitimate concern from many pastors, elders, and church leaders. As usual, clarity is found when we look through the lens of God's grand story.

We're all created in God's image. We're all sinners. We're all in need of redemption. Therefore, to help someone with a specific sin struggle, you don't have to struggle with that same sin yourself before being able to help. Actually, Satan wants to immobilize us into inaction, and this is one of his best tactics.

Still, you can be honest that you don't know personally what it's like to experience same-sex attractions and that you may not be an expert on this topic—but you want to learn. Lovingly communicate that your loved one's biggest problem is a sin nature, which is the same thing you struggle with! In God's eyes, there's nothing really extraordinary about this situation. In other words, he or she isn't much different from the rest of us.

From my doctoral research on sexuality at Christian colleges and universities, students with same-sex attractions felt that they had to suffer alone and that no one would ever understand them. No Christian should have to bear any burden by himself. Be sure to tell your loved one or friend, "You're not alone. I don't know all there is to know about this. But I know Jesus, and I want to walk with you to Jesus." These words can be life giving for someone. Feel free to be specific and ask how you can help:

- "How can I be a better friend and support you well?"
- "What are ways I can pray for you?"
- "Can we regularly pray together in person or on the phone?"
- "Is it okay for me to ask you how you're doing?"
- "Please let me know if you ever want to talk."

Whatever you commit to, be sure to follow through. Honestly, when a dear friend with same-sex attractions comes to you in his or her time of need, what your loved one needs most is not an expert but a friend—and you can be that friend.

Be Realistic

We often give the false impression that coming to Jesus means no more problems, no more struggles—as if we can just "pray away the gay." This lie has led many with same-sex attractions to "give up" on Christianity, because it didn't "work" to put an end to their struggle.

Praying and reading the Bible are vital in the life of a Christian; however, we don't read the Bible and pray so trials don't come our way. I read the Bible and pray so I'm firmly grounded in God's truth, and when— not if—difficulties come, I'm right in the path of God's grace, which empowers me to remain faithful even in the midst of temptations.

Following Jesus doesn't mean we'll no longer have inner turmoil but that even in the midst of these trials, our hope and well-being will be bound up in the certainty of God's future good for us. As I've said previously, the Christian life doesn't mean you won't be tempted; it means you have the Spirit-wrought ability to be holy even in the midst of temptations.

In reality, there was little mental turmoil before I became a Christian. I did whatever I wanted. I had an itch; I scratched it. A desire popped in my head; I did it. Now I have a heavenly Father I want to please and an enemy nipping at my heels. But the difference is that my joy is not contingent on daily circumstances or rooted in this world. My ultimate joy is fettered to the Rock, who is Jesus Christ!

Don't Focus on the Externals

What are externals? I am talking about things like mannerisms, particular ways of walking, talking, dressing, and so on. We can focus too much on these external things that we forget about the internal matters of the heart.

Unfortunately, we've taken most of our cues for masculinity and femininity from culture. Here in America, masculine means being rough, tough, unemotional, and inartistic. The quintessential man is a football player or construction worker. Yet in Asia, these two examples are considered not masculine but barbaric!

Who says that an artistic man can't be masculine? Jubal was "the father of all those who play the lyre and pipe" (Genesis 4:21). Moses led Israel in a song of victory over Egypt (Exodus 15:1–18). David was very skilled at the harp and wrote numerous psalms. He also assigned *men* to be musicians in the temple (1 Chronicles 25:1–31).

Who says that men cannot be emotional? Many of the prophets, such as Ezra, Nehemiah, and Jeremiah, were not afraid to express their emotions through tears (Ezra 10:1; Nehemiah 1:4; Lamentations 1:16). Even Jesus himself wept (John 11:35). Emotions don't indicate femininity or an absence of masculinity.

King David was known for having a heart after God. He's famous for his brave exploits—first as a shepherd boy when he singlehandedly fought lions and bears to protect his sheep, then as a youth who bravely defied the giant Goliath, and later as a warrior-king.

But David was also known for being highly sensitive, and he probably exhibited traits that our Western culture would view as inappropriate for a "real man's man." Had David grown up today, kids probably would have teased him for being effeminate, even calling him a sissy.

The ways one talks, walks, dresses, and grows hair are not the main things to focus on. The gospel is, after all, a message about receiving a new heart. When we overemphasize the externals, we can miss out on the power of the gospel and even stifle true change. Gospel change occurs from the inside out, not from the outside in.

Ask About Faith

Asking the following question will help get at the heart of the matter and is like a barometer for your loved one's spiritual health: "How does your faith fit into all this?" In other words, are they conforming their sexuality to Scripture or conforming Scripture to their sexuality? It's a battle of realities: desire versus truth. Which reality will rule their hearts?

If your loved one tells you her faith is her anchor even in the midst of trials and temptations, this reveals a commitment to live according to God's truth. You then know that your loved one is in a good place.

However, if your loved one says he's now doubting God's existence or questioning biblical sexuality, then you may need to go back to the basics—as this person needs to be evangelized in his own heart. The focus will need to turn toward outreach and evangelism as discussed in the previous chapter.

Honestly, this battle of realities is something we all deal with. Our desires are very real; however, every feeling and every thought must be filtered through the greater reality of our faith in Christ. What influences us more on a daily basis: desire or truth? Without a vibrant faith and daily renewal, no one is able to correctly process and conform desires to the will of God.

DISCIPLESHIP

Grounded in a New Identity

As I gathered my lecture notes, the joyful banter of students slowly filled the classroom as they headed to their next class or their dorm rooms. It was a beautiful spring afternoon, and understandably, the students at Moody were quick to get outside into the warm weather—except for one.

Caleb was a star student, and his passion for Jesus was one of the first things I had noticed at the beginning of the semester. Always attentive and engaged, he sat in the front row and often posed thoughtful and articulate questions. Although normally confident and cheerful, Caleb had a very different demeanor that day.

As he approached, Caleb's feet dragged a bit on the carpet, and his unfamiliar awkwardness revealed that something wasn't right. Obviously, he wanted to say something, but I saw apprehension in his eyes. With the classroom empty, I took a seat with him and asked what was on his mind.

Caleb stumbled through a few sentences and mentioned that he had wanted to talk to me for quite some time. Taking a deep breath, he finally mustered up enough courage to get out what he had come to say. For the first time in his life, Caleb confided in someone about the reality of his same-sex attractions. This brave confession turned out to be a notable point in Caleb's journey as a man of God.

The exact scenario and details may have differed, but this sort of conversation wasn't unique for me. Many young men and women similar to Caleb have opened up to me about their struggles with same-sex attractions. Most had never acted on those feelings, but they were alone bearing this burden.

Is Caleb's story similar to your story? Do you experience same-sex attractions? Are you struggling alone? Are you weighed down with guilt and shame? This much is true: one of Satan's best weapons is isolation.

No More Shame

Shame can be debilitating. For many Christians who have same-sex attractions, guilt is a common reality. Some may have already acted on their feelings in an inappropriate sexual or emotional relationship. Others may feel immense guilt for simply being tempted in this way.

Erwin Lutzer, pastor emeritus of the Moody Church, has provided noteworthy insight on guilt. He explains that guilt is actually good, but it has one purpose—to lead us to confess and repent of our sin. Once we confess and repent, we can cling to the promise of 1 John 1:9: "If we confess our sins, he is faithful and just to forgive us our sins and to cleanse us from all unrighteousness."

Therefore, once the purpose of guilt has been accomplished, there is no more need for it. Unfortunately, when it comes to shame, most Christians cannot discern between the prompting of the Holy Spirit and the accusations of the Enemy. Lutzer describes it best:

> The Holy Spirit convicts us for sins that we have been unwilling
> to face in God's presence; Satan makes us feel guilty for sins that
> are already "under the blood of Christ," that is, for sins that we
> have already confessed. The Holy Spirit reminds us of our sins

before we are cleansed; Satan continues to remind us of them *after* we are cleansed.[1]

If you've sinned in the past—whether through sexual activity or lustful thoughts—and you've confessed and repented, then the feelings of guilt you're having are not from God but from the Enemy.

However, if you've sinned and you haven't confessed and repented, then the Holy Spirit is prompting you to do so and receive God's gift of forgiveness! Please heed the Spirit's conviction. If you confess, our Father's pardon and cleansing are guaranteed!

I also know that you may be weighed down by anxiety about what the future may hold for you. You may think, *How can I continue like this forever? I can't be single for the rest of my life—it's too difficult being alone!* Just as you shouldn't be weighed down by the guilt of sins that you've already confessed and repented of, you also shouldn't be weighed down by anxiety about the future.

Jesus provides some excellent wisdom that should be our daily reminder: "Do not be anxious about tomorrow, for tomorrow will be anxious for itself" (Matthew 6:34). We cannot change a thing through worry, yet we still fret. If God is in control, he has tomorrow already planned—with you in mind!

Actually, we should live with blinders, as horses do. But instead of blinders for the left and right, we need blinders for the back and front, our past shame and future anxiety. God doesn't want us to be weighed down with undue guilt and worry. He desires that we focus on the now, live for today. When you think these thoughts of shame and anxiety, remember that they're not coming from God but from the Enemy. Your response should be, "Get behind me, Satan!"

Once we've confessed and repented, we are free from guilt. We're ready to move forward in our journey, and a key aspect of growing in

Christ is discipleship. But you might say, "I don't have a mentor." Start with prayer for one and ask God to provide. Be observant and watch people around you in your local church where you attend and are hopefully a member.

Look for godly qualities in people you admire and respect. Don't be afraid to ask one of your pastors, an elder, deacon, or church leader to be your mentor. Just as I explained in the chapter on spiritual family, you don't have to find someone just like you or who also experiences same-sex attractions to disciple you. The diversity of the body of Christ is a beautiful thing. I personally have learned so much from godly mentors who were different than I—but they deeply loved Jesus.

Also, don't be discouraged if the first one you ask says he or she is too busy or has another reason. Don't give up. Keep asking until God provides. He will provide, because he does not withhold good gifts from those who seek.

Follow Me

Discipleship begins when we respond to these two words: "Follow me." For three years, the twelve disciples followed Jesus—they watched, learned, and grew. The Greek word for "disciple" is *mathetes,* which means "one who engages in learning." Thus, a good "learner" is humble, teachable, and able to receive correction.

Peer-to-peer relationships are very important in the life of a Christian. Accountability among Christian brothers or sisters is good, yet it's limited in its effectiveness because peer accountability has no spiritual headship. Remember, friendship isn't equivalent to discipleship.

Discipleship is with someone in a position of authority, like a mentor or teacher. In Titus 2, Paul exhorts older women to train young women.

Older men are to be an example and to teach younger men. To be a disciple means spending time with the "teacher."

The twelve disciples simply did life together with Jesus. You may not be able to follow someone around for three years, but you can commit to intentionally and consistently connecting with your mentor one on one or in a small discipleship group.

Scripture and Church

Everywhere Jesus went, he preached and taught with authority. Discipleship is grounded in Scripture: "For the word of God is living and active, sharper than any two-edged sword, piercing to the division of soul and of spirit, of joints and of marrow, and discerning the thoughts and intentions of the heart" (Hebrews 4:12).

For me and my parents, the one common thread of conversion is God's Word. My mother was mentored for six weeks immediately following her conversion, which was like an intensive Bible retreat. My father came to know Christ through Bible Study Fellowship. I found the Bible in a trash can, and my time in prison flew by as I read through it several times. The discipleship relationship should always be based on the study of and submission to Scripture.

In addition, the correct context for discipleship is the local church. Unfortunately, many approaches to ministering to individuals with same-sex attractions may include building intentional friendships, counseling, or support groups. For many of these parachurch organizations, *true* discipleship receives little or no emphasis. Friendship is not discipleship; neither is discipleship the same as counseling or a support group.

Here is what Mark Dever, senior pastor of the Capitol Hill Baptist

Church in Washington, DC, has to say about the prominence of the local church in discipleship:

> The local church—this Father-designed, Jesus-authorized, and Spirit-gifted body—is far better equipped to undertake the work of discipling believers than simply you and your one friend. Jesus does not promise that you and your one friend will defeat the gates of hell. He promises that the church will do this. You cannot recognize yourself as gifted and called to teach God's Word, or to baptize and administer the Lord's Supper, like a local church is so authorized.[2]

The local church should not be an afterthought or, worse, ignored. The local church means the proclamation of truth, the ordinances and sacraments, community, accountability, redemptive discipline, forgiveness, and restoration. Ground yourself in the local church and make it your home. Local church membership should be a reality of every believer.

Imitate Christ

At the heart of discipleship is the call for all believers to emulate Christ and to conform our lives to his. Thus, we imitate Christ in his servanthood (John 13:14), in his love (John 13:34), in his suffering (1 Peter 2:21), and in his obedience (1 John 2:6). In addition, we are also "predestined to be conformed to the image of his Son" (Romans 8:29). The Bible declares that Jesus is the end goal of discipleship.

Imitating Christ in discipleship means living out and tangibly expressing the profound reality of our union with Christ. As believers, we are created in Christ (Ephesians 2:10), crucified with Christ (Galatians 2:20), buried with Christ (Colossians 2:12), baptized into Christ and his death (Romans 6:3), and united with Christ in his resurrection (Romans 6:5). Moreover, we are justified in Christ (Romans 3:24), glorified in Christ (Romans 8:30), and sanctified in Christ (1 Corinthians 1:2). This is what I mean by identity in Christ.

As such, I do not put my identity in my sexuality. My identity is not gay, ex-gay, or even heterosexual for that matter. As one who is united with Christ, I do not identify with my same-sex sexual and romantic desires that are a result of the Fall. These desires are not neutral or sanctifiable but arise from my sin nature—and therefore must be put to death every day.

Sinful desires and temptations may seem like an integral aspect of who you are, so you will need mentors and siblings to lovingly and persistently remind you to deny yourself and pick up your cross daily. The gospel is costly, but it's worth it!

At the end of the day, our sexuality is not the biggest issue. The biggest issue for all of us—same-sex attracted, opposite-sex attracted, or both—is whether we're truly following Christ or not. Following Jesus is the goal. Our destination must be Christ.

The clearest articulation of following Jesus is found in all three Synoptic Gospels. Jesus explains the cost of discipleship: "If anyone would come after me, let him deny himself and take up his cross daily and follow me. For whoever would save his life will lose it, but whoever loses his life for my sake will save it" (Luke 9:23–24; Matthew 16:24–25; Mark 8:34–35).

We want to follow Jesus without denying ourselves and taking up our cross daily. That's not possible. We convince ourselves that denying our desires, our thoughts, and even our sexuality is optional. However,

Jesus spoke this truth not only for superspiritual Christians; this is for "anyone" who wants to "come after me." Following Jesus should cost us everything; if it hasn't, you're following the wrong Jesus.

One of my favorite verses comes from the prophet Habakkuk:

> Though the fig tree should not blossom, nor fruit be on the vines, the produce of the olive fail and the fields yield no food, the flock be cut off from the fold and there be no herd in the stalls, yet I will rejoice in the LORD; I will take joy in the God of my salvation. (Habakkuk 3:17–18)

God has had a habit of pruning things away in my life—even some that were good yet not of ultimate and eternal importance. Heed these words from our Savior, "And everyone who has left houses or brothers or sisters or father or mother or children or lands, for my name's sake, will receive a hundredfold and inherit eternal life" (Matthew 19:29). "For my name's sake" indicates that all our losses and all our gains can be understood only when Christ is our final destination.

In 1952 Florence Chadwick was the only woman to have swum the English Channel in both directions—also breaking the world record while doing so. She planned a new challenge: to swim the twenty-six miles from Catalina Island to the coast of Southern California. She trained for months in preparation for this difficult swim.

Florence went to the island one early morning. She was flanked by small boats with her mom, coach, and a few others. They watched for sharks and prepared to help her if she got tired or hurt. She went into the cold water covered with grease to stay warm and began to swim. She swam and swam and swam.

Fifteen hours later, the fog rolled in, and Florence could barely see anything in front of her. The water was getting colder, and her legs were cramping. She began to doubt her ability. Her mother kept trying to encourage and cheer her on: "You can do this. You've trained hard for this."

After a little while, though, Florence gave up. When they pulled her out of the water into the boat, they told her she was only one mile away from the coast.

Florence did not give up on her dream. She resumed her training program, and two months later, early one morning she went back to the island. Just like the first time, she was flanked by small boats with her mom, coach, and others. She covered herself with grease and began to swim. She swam and swam and swam.

Fifteen hours later, the fog rolled in just as it had the first time. She couldn't see anything in front of her. The water got colder, and her legs cramped. She began to doubt her ability, but her mother told her to keep going. "You can do this!" Florence swam on. Finally she made it to the shoreline.

When she got out of the water, many reporters were waiting and asked her how she was able to make it with all the fog and the same conditions. Florence's response was profound: "I kept a mental picture of the California coastline in my mind." With every stroke she took, she kept her gaze on her destination. She never lost sight of her end goal. Florence's focus was on the finish line.[3]

As Florence swam, her focus wasn't behind her. She did not look back at the miles she had just covered. Surely her strokes could've been more efficient. She should've paced herself better. But in order to finish, she had to keep her focus on the end goal.

Paul says in Philippians 3:13–14, "Brothers, I do not consider that I have made it my own. But one thing I do: forgetting what lies behind and straining forward to what lies ahead, I press on toward the goal for the prize of the upward call of God in Christ Jesus." Remember, our biggest problem is not our past hurts or traumas. Our biggest problem is our sin nature, and victory is found only in Christ Jesus.

As Florence swam, her focus also wasn't to the side. Her mother and coach provided words of encouragement. But if Florence had put all her attention on her mom and coach, she would have lost sight of her goal. When we put so much focus on our friends or loved ones as the main answer to our ailments, we really make the second commandment (love of neighbor) the greatest commandment (love of God). The ultimate goal of all earthly relationships should be to help us "love the Lord your God with all your heart and with all your soul and with all your strength and with all your mind" (Luke 10:27).

As Florence swam, her focus wasn't on her circumstances. The water was frigid. The waves were choppy. The fog was thick. The ocean was deep. But if she had fixated on her situation, she would have lost sight of her final destination. When Jesus called Peter out on the water, Peter moved his gaze away from the Lord and onto his circumstances: "When he saw the wind, he was afraid, and beginning to sink he cried out, 'Lord, save me'" (Matthew 14:30).

Trials will come for everyone—whether it's loneliness as a single individual or the fierce struggle of putting to death indwelling sin. But if we focus only on our circumstances and lose sight of Christ, we will sink. Whatever we are going through, we must look to Jesus and fix our eyes on him since he is the founder and perfecter of our faith (Hebrews 12:2).

Jesus can be seen in every key element of God's grand story—creation, fall, redemption, and consummation. In the beginning, God created all things through Christ and for Christ (Colossians 1:16). When Adam and Eve fell, God cursed the serpent and foretold that Jesus, as the "offspring" of the woman, would one day bruise Satan's head (Genesis 3:15).

Redemption is only through the blood of Jesus, and we have been redeemed from the curse of the law because Christ became a curse for us (Ephesians 1:7; Galatians 3:13). On the last day, all the redeemed will have their names read from the Lamb's book of life, and the marriage between Christ and his bride, the church, will be fully consummated in glory (Revelation 19:7; 21:27).

If sex, desire, and relationships are shaped by God's grand story and God's grand story is shaped by Christ, then this means that sex, desire, and relationships—our whole sexuality—must be shaped by Christ as well. All my sexual behaviors, erotic desires, romantic feelings, sentimental relationships, and even all my platonic friendships must be conformed to Jesus Christ and nothing else.

Jesus Christ is our destination. He is our end goal. Let us fix our eyes on Jesus. We are running the race and striving to cross the finish line. The family of the redeemed stand in the risen Christ alone. Our finish line is Christ. It is for this reality I live. It is for this reality I'm willing to die. And it is for this reality I wrote this book.

Study Guide

The concept of holy sexuality should challenge each of us to examine God's will for our lives. How do we evaluate our desires and relationships in light of the gospel? How is our identity shaped by God's grand story—creation, fall, redemption, and consummation?

This eight-week study guide will help you examine these topics more deeply and in a more focused manner through discussion with friends, family, or a small group. Each week in the study guide includes eight to thirteen questions based on two or three chapters from the book.

Go through all the questions, or pick and choose which questions fit your group or situation best. In addition, feel free to highlight as you read and add questions of your own. The purpose is to develop a more profound relationship with Christ as you explore the biblical and theological aspects of holy sexuality.

WEEK 1

Read chapters 1–3 before discussion.

1. What drew you to read about the topic of holy sexuality? Have you read other books on this topic from a Christian perspective? How do you hope to benefit from reading this book?

2. Considering how to show compassion for our loved ones who experience same-sex attractions, Dr. Yuan asks, "What does this love look like?" Think about a time when you experienced compassionate love. What did it look like? (Chapter 1)

3. In terms of the church's historical approach to ministering to those with same-sex attractions, Dr. Yuan asks, "Could the gospel be calling us *all* to something costlier and more magnificent than we've ever envisioned?" What do you think? (Chapter 1)

4. If we rush into doing "what's right" without first establishing *right thinking,* there's a good chance we could actually be doing what's wrong. How have you seen this displayed in the way Christians have handled the issue of homosexuality (or any other issue) in the past? What, in your opinion, is the best way forward? (Chapter 1)

5. Dr. Yuan states that the goal of this book is "to provide both theological reflection on sexuality and practical action points for those of us trying to share Christ with our gay loved ones through the lens of God's grand story." Can you explain God's grand story—creation, fall, redemption, and consummation? What are your thoughts about theology and its relevance to your own life? What does it mean to think of theology as a verb? (Chapter 1)

6. Andy was a classmate of Dr. Yuan who said, "This is who I am." Do you know someone like Andy? Without giving a name, how has this person's "essence" affected his "ethics"? Have you noted in someone that her understanding of who she is has affected how she thinks and lives? (Chapter 2)

7. When asked to introduce yourself, what do you say? Read John 1:12–13 and Acts 17:28. How does God describe our identity? Why do you think so many view sexuality as "who they are" rather than something they feel or do? (Chapter 2)

8. Briefly explain the philosophies of existentialism and nihilism. How have they led to a vacuum in our culture where experience has become the most valued authority in a person's life? What other worldviews do you see present in our culture today? (Chapter 2)

9. How does John Calvin's statement that "man never achieves a clear knowledge of himself unless he has first looked upon God's face" contradict the generally accepted modern understanding of self? How would you explain the term *theological anthropology* to someone? (Chapter 2)

10. The two most important aspects of theological anthropology are the image of God and the doctrine of sin. Dr. Yuan explains, "The image of God without the Fall leads to universalism (the belief that all humanity is eventually granted eternal life with God), while the doctrine of sin without the *imago Dei* leads to legalistic moralism." We often err on one side (all grace) or the other (all truth). Can you tell of a time when this was true in your own life? (Chapter 3)

11. Moisés Silva said, "*Every* aspect of human beings is a reflection of the divine image." Bruce Waltke said that we're "made like God so that God can communicate himself to people." How have you heard others describe the image of God? Has your understanding changed? In what way is the *imago Dei* the only true foundation of human rights? (Chapter 3)

12. Many people have argued that same-sex relationships are "natural." Give a couple more examples of things animals do that humans should not copy. How is this an example of low anthropology? (Chapter 3)

13. Our being made male or female is an essential part of the *imago Dei*. Review Genesis 1:27. Explain to each other the poetic structure and parallel between the three lines and the connection between the image of God and male and female. Dr. Yuan wrote, "Transgenderism is not only a battle of ontology (the study of being) but also a battle of epistemology (the study of knowledge)." Explain what this means to you. (Chapter 3)

WEEK 2

Read chapters 4–5 before discussion.

1. John Frame said, "If we abandon the Christian belief that we fell in Adam, by what right do we maintain that we are saved in Christ?" Why is a proper understanding of the doctrine of sin essential to understanding who we are? In what way is it an integral aspect of understanding holy sexuality? (Chapter 4)

2. What was the purpose of the tree of the knowledge of good and evil in the Garden of Eden? How was this a gift from God, not a temptation? (Chapter 4)

3. Dr. Yuan asserts that the orthodox doctrine of sin is offensive to many because it's difficult to accept that you're guilty of something you didn't do (referring back to Adam's sin). How do you respond to this? Do you have a tendency to feel defensive? Do you think it's fair for God to hold us to his perfect standard? Why is it critical that we look to Jesus when trying to understand sin, guilt, and corruption? (Chapter 4)

4. In light of Galatians 5:16–17, how does being born again free us from bondage to original sin? How do we fight against "indwelling sin" after conversion? What effect does the battle against our flesh have on our sexuality? (Chapter 4)

5. Consider and discuss the difference between "able to sin and able not to sin" and "unable not to sin." How does this distinction apply to humanity at creation, after the Fall, and as redeemed followers of Christ? (Chapter 4)

6. Do you know of Christians who have a "holier than thou" attitude toward gays and lesbians that reflects arrogant condemnation? What are ways we can respond to them? Is there any way we can help them understand God's grace? (Chapter 5)

7. Dr. Yuan lists some of the "root causes" of same-sex attractions commonly mentioned among Christians: absentee father, dominant mother, past trauma, etc. Yet in no other sin struggle is the blame put so squarely on the shoulders of the parents. Have you seen this to be true in your own community? What does Dr. Yuan say is the actual root of same-sex attractions? Do you agree? (Chapter 5)

8. How can you help someone with same-sex attraction if you don't personally struggle with it? Tell about an instance when someone struggling with sin was ministered to by another who didn't struggle with the same sin. (Chapter 5)

9. Discuss the difference between a natural consequence of the Fall (like a disability or disease) and a moral consequence of the Fall (like greed, envy, or hatred). Which is same-sex attraction? Why is this important? (Chapter 5)

10. Some argue that people are born gay so it's okay. Is this a biblical approach to the issue? How do the concepts of original sin and being born again influence your understanding of being "born gay"? How would you respond if someone said people are born gay? (Chapter 5)

WEEK 3

Read chapters 6–8 before discussion.

1. How would you define a "normal" human life experience? A "normal" Christian life experience? Why is being "normal" an incorrect goal for us to have? How is it different from a biblical sexual ethic? Can you think of other "normal" behaviors that are actually sinful? (Chapter 6)

2. Define *sexuality* in your own words. How does Dr. Yuan define it? He wrote, "Heterosexuality is *not* synonymous with biblical

marriage." What does this mean? What is the opposite of hetero-sexuality? Use your own words to explain this. (Chapter 6)

3. Describe the concept of holy sexuality, specifically the two paths. What are your thoughts on the concept of these two paths? Do you agree? (Chapter 6)

4. Is sexual desire truly a prerequisite (or even a requirement) for marriage? Or is an erotic "litmus test" a lie born in the sexual revolution that has tainted a biblical concept of marriage? (Chapter 6)

5. Before reading this book, did you think that same-sex attractions were sinful or not? After reading this chapter, what are your thoughts about this question? (Chapter 7)

6. Have you seen people argue and debate without defining terms? Why is defining important? How could it have helped the conversation? Can you think of other terms related to sexuality and the Christian faith that need to be defined? (Chapter 7)

7. Dr. Yuan explains that "tempt" and "test" are the same word in Greek. God tests us to sharpen our character. Satan tempts us to sin and disobey God. Puritan pastor John Owen said, "Temptation is like a knife, that may either cut the meat or the throat of a man; it may be his food or his poison, his exercise or his destruction." Explain what this statement means to you. (Chapter 7)

8. Read 1 Corinthians 10:13 and Hebrews 2:18. Discuss both Bible verses in light of your own temptations. How do they encourage you? How do they strengthen you? What is our "escape hatch" from temptation? Talk about how these implications affect your relationships with those with same-sex attractions. (Chapter 7)

9. Do you feel as if the church has promoted the fallacy that a "good Christian" is somehow immune from temptation? Do you feel

freedom to admit the temptations you struggle with, or do you feel you need to keep them private, shared only with a select, trusted few? How can we make our local churches a safer and more redemptive place for those wrestling with same-sex temptations or any other temptation? What do you plan to do to make the church safer and more redemptive? (Chapter 7)

10. Saint Augustine prayed, "You have made us for Yourself, and our hearts are restless until they rest in You." He also wrote, "The whole life of a good Christian is an holy desire." Now read Psalm 73:25; Hosea 6:6; John 17:24; Romans 10:1; and 1 Timothy 2:4. Take a few minutes to write down a personal statement about your own desire. Share with the group either what your desire is or what you learned about yourself by focusing on one primary desire of your heart. How does it influence the rest of your life? (Chapter 8)

11. Dr. Yuan says that "all desire is *teleological*." All desire is about something and has an intended action. Can you give more examples of a desire, its object, and its intended action? In light of a desire's "end," what is the litmus test to discern between good and bad desires? (Chapter 8)

12. Explain the difference between sexual desire, romantic desire, and platonic desire. Keeping in mind these three types of desires, what sort of desires contribute to sexuality, and what sort do not? (Chapter 8)

13. The analogy was made between same-sex romantic desires and a married man developing a romantic relationship with a woman not his wife. Do you know anyone who developed romantic desires for another that led down the wrong path? What are ways to help prevent situations like that? (Chapter 8)

WEEK 4

Read chapters 9–11 before discussion.

1. What are the key elements of a secular paradigm of sexual orientation? How do you understand the orientation we all have for sin? When did this sinful orientation begin in all of us? Is this sinful orientation in all of us chosen? Will this sinful orientation ever go away on this side of heaven? (Chapter 9)

2. In Galatians 5:16–17, Paul explains that the flesh fights against the Spirit and the Spirit fights against the flesh. How have you seen this in your own life? What would this look like for a same-sex-attracted Christian? Does this give you more empathy for someone with this struggle, and how would you communicate this common reality with someone struggling with same-sex attractions? (Chapter 9)

3. Read Ephesians 4:22–24. Dr. Yuan argues, "Christ's salvific work certainly has inaugurated a new era, but this new era is also not fully consummated." How have you experienced the conflict between the flesh and the Spirit as you live in the "already but not yet"? How does grace play a part in this conflict? (Chapter 9)

4. Think about the most recent wedding you've attended (or your own wedding if you're married). In that ceremony and celebration, what stands out as most meaningful to you? How and to what extent did the wedding reflect a biblical vision of the union of husband and wife? What is your idea of a perfect Christian and God-centered wedding? How do we celebrate the union of a husband and a wife without putting God on the back burner and oversentimentalizing marriage? (Chapter 10)

5. Dr. Yuan says that "the most deceptive form of idolatry is when we worship something good." Can you think of any good things that we idolize? The Supreme Court in its decision on gay marriage said,

"No union is more profound than marriage, for it embodies the highest ideals of love, fidelity, devotion, sacrifice, and family." Dr. Yuan says he respectfully but resolutely disagrees. What do you think? (Chapter 10)

6. What are your thoughts on whether marriage is the cure for loneliness? What other forms of loving and God-honoring relationships can help us meet our need for companionship? How can we celebrate the sacred union of biblical marriage in light of Jesus being unmarried here on earth? (Chapter 10)

7. Read Genesis 2:18. In the past, how did you understand Eve's role as "helper"? Now read Genesis 2:15 and Psalm 121:1–2. How do these passages help you understand the meaning and role of "helper"? How do these implications affect your understanding of marriage in general or your own marriage (if you're married)? (Chapter 10)

8. Dr. Yuan explains that in Genesis 2:18 "helper fit for him" refers to both similarity and dissimilarity. Read Genesis 1:27 and 2:24, taking note of the separating and binding. Now go through Genesis 1–2 and discuss the other examples of similarity and dissimilarity, separating and binding. (Chapter 10)

9. The children's answers to the question "What is love?" are really adorable. How would you answer the question? How does your answer compare with the way the world would answer this question? Read Romans 5:8; 1 John 4:10; and 2 John 6. How does the Bible answer this question? (Chapter 11)

10. Read Matthew 19:3–6 and Mark 10:2–9. Now read Genesis 1:27 and 2:24. What does the term *one flesh* mean, and why is it important? Why is sexual differentiation in marriage—one man and one woman—paramount in light of Genesis 1:27 and the concept of *imago Dei*? (Chapter 11)

11. It's often asserted that Jesus was silent about homosexuality. Do a mock situation and practice how you would explain to each other Jesus's teaching on marriage in Matthew 19 and Mark 10, which is from Genesis 1 and 2. (Chapter 11)

12. Read Ephesians 5:25–33. Now read Matthew 22:29–32; Mark 12:24–27; and Luke 20:34–38. Dr. Yuan tells about pastor Ken Smith, who recently became a widower. Express your thoughts about marriage in light of eternity after reading these Bible passages and Pastor Ken's words. (Chapter 11)

WEEK 5

Read chapters 12–13 before discussion.

1. Do you believe singleness is cast in a negative light in our culture in general? Do you believe singleness is cast in a negative light in the church? Why or why not? (Chapter 12)

2. How have you seen your church respond positively to singleness? How can our churches improve in having a more biblical view of singleness and not treating single individuals like projects to be fixed? What does a deficient view of singleness have to do with your gay friends? (Chapter 12)

3. Those who have never been married do not have any offspring. Explain how the Old Testament portrays the individual without any offspring. How does Jesus, who was unmarried without any physical offspring, "dramatically redefine the family" with the inauguration of the new covenant? (Chapter 12)

4. Read Matthew 19:3–12. Dr. Yuan makes note that the end of verse 12, "Let the one who is able to receive this receive it," must be read together with verse 11, "Not everyone can receive this saying." What is "this saying"? In this verse, how does Jesus affirm that

both biblical marriage and biblical singleness are good things for his
followers? Are you able to "receive" or understand that being single
can be advantageous, just as being married can be advantageous?
(Chapter 13)

5. Read Luke 20:34–36. From these verses we see that sex and
marriage are not eternal fixtures in God's grand story. What are
your thoughts about this? How has this affected the way you
understand sexuality? (Chapter 13)

6. Barry Danylak explains, "Married people are necessary because the
church is still part of the current age, but single people remind us
that the spiritual age has already been inaugurated in Christ and
awaits imminent consummation." Discuss the "already but not yet"
that we're living in. What other examples, besides marriage, can
you think of that show this dichotomy? (Chapter 13)

7. Dr. Yuan explains several examples of how the gift of singleness has
been misunderstood: it is not a vocation, not necessarily lifelong,
not a special capacity for enjoying singleness, not continence, and
not a spiritual gift. Did any of these surprise you? Which ones and
why? (Chapter 13)

8. Unlike spiritual gifts that enable the believer to *do* certain things
empowered by the Holy Spirit, the gift of singleness is simply good.
Can you think of a few examples of how singleness can be good?
(Chapter 13)

WEEK 6

Read chapters 14–15 before discussion.

1. David and Jonathan had a strong love for each other. Read 1 Samuel
18:1, 3–4; 20:41; and 2 Samuel 1:26. Our culture has programmed
us to assume that the love between two men must always be sexual.

Give a few examples where you have seen this wrong assumption being made. (Chapter 14)

2. John Piper writes, "I am declaring the temporary and secondary nature of marriage and family over against the eternal and primary nature of the church." Dr. Yuan elevates the "new family" that is the church and explains that "entrance into this new family is not through physical birth but through spiritual rebirth." What are specific ways that our local churches can improve in living out this reality? (Chapter 14)

3. Do you know of individuals who claim to be Christians but believe that being a part of the local church is unnecessary? How would you explain the necessity of the local body of Christ, the church? How can the church become a place of accountability and discipline, forgiveness and restoration, wholeness and integration not only for persons who experience same-sex attraction but for all God's people? (Chapter 14)

4. Are we as the church doing family well? Is this a lived-out reality for you? Are the youth in your community learning from the older saints? Are the young couples and singles learning from the godly single or married elderly women and men, and vice versa? Explain two specific ways in which the local church can make this more of a reality. (Chapter 14)

5. Dr. Yuan says this about integration: "It's much harder—and sometimes inappropriate—for a single person to invite himself into the life and home of a family. But it's completely appropriate for a husband and wife to invite a single sister or brother into the regular life of the couple's home." If you are married (with or without children), what will you do this month to make a single Christian brother or sister know that you are all part of the same family? (Chapter 14)

6. Dr. Yuan tells the story of Michelangelo creating the statue *David* by simply carving away everything that "wasn't David" from the block of marble. How is this a good illustration of the way the Christian life should work? (Chapter 15)

7. Read 2 Corinthians 5:17. If a Christian is still tempted by same-sex sexual desire, does this mean no true transformation has occurred in the person's soul? No healing and deliverance? Do temptations to other sin indicate that no transformation has happened? (Chapter 15)

8. Dr. Yuan says this: "The process of being made holy is a radical, inward transformation flowing from our union with Christ. God's gracious gift of sanctification should be permeating the whole person—our thoughts, desires, and actions. *This is gospel holiness.*" Describe the process of sanctification in your own life. (Chapter 15)

9. What is the difference between justification and sanctification? How has the misunderstanding of the two led to the fact that many people who consider themselves Christians are not on the path of sanctification? (Chapter 15)

WEEK 7

Read chapters 16–17 before discussion.

1. Read Matthew 7:15. Wolves in sheep's clothing are hard to detect. Have you ever been deceived, or have you known someone who was deceived? Tell about that situation. How could it have been avoided? (Chapter 16)

2. Now read the whole passage, Matthew 7:15–20. How is Matthew Vines's critique of the church as a "bad tree" flawed? How does Scripture tell us to distinguish "good fruit" from "bad fruit"? What

is the mistake in Matthew Vines's interpretation of the "bad fruit"? (Chapter 16)

3. Suicidality and depression are often aggravated when an individual suffers alone. What is a good response from a theologically sound Christian to the suffering of someone with same-sex attractions? What have you done or what do you plan to do to help make the body of Christ a more redemptive and safe place for the person with same-sex attractions or for anyone struggling alone? (Chapter 16)

4. Dr. Yuan's parents first knew that they were sinners, which put things in perspective and enabled them to love Jordan, Dr. Yuan's gay friend. Why do you think that knowing we're sinners helps us love others? (Chapter 17)

5. Dr. Yuan suggests that parables are written to provoke us out of our comfort zone and make us consider, *What still needs to be changed in my life?* Has this ever happened for you when reading one of Jesus's parables? Or when reading any other Bible story in the Old or New Testaments? (Chapter 17)

6. With the parable of the good Samaritan, the important thing is to put ourselves in the shoes of the man who was robbed. After you read the parable in this way, using the text below, explain your thoughts and feelings. What would you think upon waking up from your coma and finding out a Samaritan cared for you? How would this affect the way you answered the question, "Who is my neighbor?" (Chapter 17)

I was going down from Jerusalem to Jericho, and *I* fell among robbers, who stripped *me* and beat *me* and departed, leaving *me* half dead. Now by chance a priest was going down that road, and when he saw *me* he passed by on the other side. So likewise a Levite, when he came to the place and saw *me*, passed by on

the other side. But a Samaritan, as he journeyed, came to where
I was, and when he saw *me,* he had compassion. He went to *me*
and bound up *my* wounds, pouring on oil and wine. Then he set
me on his own animal and brought *me* to an inn and took care of
me. And the next day he took out two denarii and gave them to
the innkeeper, saying, "Take care of *this individual,* and whatever
more you spend, I will repay you when I come back."

7. Jesus teaches that the second commandment is "You shall love
your neighbor as yourself" (Matthew 22:39). Think of your friend
or relative who identifies as gay or a coworker or neighbor. What
specific and tangible things can you do this week to show this
person love? Commit to doing them, and report back next week
about the outcome. (Chapter 17)

8. How can the body of Christ be a safer and more redemptive place?
Can you think of an example when a person opened up about
something and it turned out negatively? Can you think of another
example when a person opened up about something and it turned
out positively? What active steps can we take to make more positive
situations happen? (Chapter 17)

WEEK 8

Read chapters 18–20 before discussion.

1. Do you know any missionaries who are in Muslim closed countries? If you had a devout Muslim neighbor or coworker, when
would you bring up your theological differences? In what ways
can we learn from our evangelism strategies with Muslims and
apply them to our interactions with gay friends and loved ones?
(Chapter 18)

2. Dr. Yuan first lists the things we should avoid. Have you ever done any of these things? Several have to do with things we shouldn't say. What could we say instead? We also shouldn't debate. Can you think of some good responses to these difficult questions posed by our gay friends? "Do you think being gay is a sin?" "Do you think I'm going to hell?" "Why would God make me this way and not allow me to be who I am?" (Chapter 18)

3. Dr. Yuan's mom, Angela, fasted every Monday for eight years. Have you ever tried fasting before? What are your fears? Tell us about a time that you fasted. What did you learn from it? Did you know that fasting is not always about food? What could you fast from other than food? Will you try to fast once in the next three months? If it is your first time, fast for only one or two meals. (Chapter 18)

4. One suggestion is to be transparent and share what God has done in your life. Briefly share your testimony. Also tell about something God has done in your life this past year. (Chapter 18)

5. Paul writes, "Bear one another's burdens, and so fulfill the law of Christ" (Galatians 6:2). If a dear friend confides in you about the reality of experiencing same-sex attractions, along with the advice Dr. Yuan provides, what else would you do or say? (Chapter 19)

6. Dr. Yuan states that we often give the false impression that coming to Jesus means we'll have no more problems. Ever since you became a Christian, have things been a cakewalk for you? Explain a particular period in which things were difficult. Feel free to share something that may be difficult in your life now. Hebrews 11:1 reads, "Now faith is the assurance of things hoped for, the conviction of things not seen." How has God given you hope in the midst of your storm? (Chapter 19)

7. From our childhood, we're taught not to judge a book by its cover—yet we still do. Can you recall a time when you were judged by the way you acted? Maybe even teased for being gay? Do you know of someone who might not fit the typical masculine or feminine mold but who does not identify as gay or even experience same-sex attractions (that you're aware of)? Without confusing them with *male* and *female,* what do *masculine* and *feminine* mean to you? (Chapter 19)

8. When a close friend confides in you that she has same-sex attractions, it's very important to ask how faith fits in. How does faith fit into your daily life? How does it fit in with your work? How does it fit in on a daily basis in your home life with your spouse and kids (if you're married and a parent)? How does it fit in with your interests or hobbies? (Chapter 19)

9. Erwin Lutzer explains, "The Holy Spirit convicts us for sins that we have been unwilling to face in God's presence; Satan makes us feel guilty for sins that are already 'under the blood of Christ,' that is, for sins that we have already confessed." Have you ever felt guilt about something God has already forgiven you for? What was it? Have you seen this conviction from the Holy Spirit or undue guilt from Satan in a friend? (Chapter 20)

10. Have you ever had a mentor and been a disciple? Who was your mentor, and what are some things you learned? Have you ever mentored someone? How was that experience? Did you learn anything from it? If you don't have a mentor or a disciple, think of someone who could be a mentor or a disciple. Approach that individual this month and ask whether he or she is willing to journey with you. (Chapter 20)

11. Scripture and the local church are essential aspects of the life of a disciple of Jesus. Tell about a recent or past sermon you heard that

had a powerful impact on you. What was it about? How did it affect you? What did you change in your thinking or in your behavior because of it? (Chapter 20)

12. Read from all three parallel passages: Matthew 16:24–25; Mark 8:34–35; and Luke 9:23–24. Explain what you think these passages mean. Whom do these passages apply to? How can you pick up your cross daily this week? (Chapter 20)

13. What has been your overall takeaway from this book and small-group discussion?

Acknowledgments

"Writing a book is like giving birth." You may have heard this old adage before, and as a single man, this is the closest thing I've experienced to having a child. Since 2015, I've been working on this book. I had a pretty rough start trying to bring structure to all that I wanted to say. Normally, writing a book shouldn't take this long, and I certainly expected to be finished in much less time.

However, with a baby, no matter what—aside from complications—a little girl or little boy is delivered in nine months. Ready or not! I won't pretend I know the pain of bearing a child for nine months or the excruciating agony of labor. But during my three years of "childbearing" (research and writing), I surely experienced pain and agony! Without all the help I received, this book would not have been possible.

More than anything else, I must begin by praising God for placing me on this journey of sweet surrender to the Lord Jesus. He has given me the courage and wisdom to put these words together. Thank you, Lord, for your patience. Continue to renew my mind to conform to the image of Christ. Empower me to deny myself and pick up my cross daily. Strengthen me to follow Jesus every moment of my life. I look forward to that day when I can see you face to face and hear you say, "Well done, good and faithful servant."

Thanks to my literary agents, Robert Wolgemuth and Austin Wilson. Robert, it was serendipitous that I had a chance to meet you in 2013. You saw potential in me, and only two years after the release of my first book in 2011—when I didn't feel like writing—you gently nudged me to be an author again. Austin, who would have known that one of my students in my second year of teaching at Moody would represent me for this book project? Your diligence in the particulars and passion for the Lord will get you far. Keep fighting the good fight!

Lawrence Kimbrough, I appreciate your helping me organize my hurricane of thoughts and ideas. Kate Etue, your eye to the manuscript and editorial talent immensely improved my writing. Like with my first book, I owe a debt of gratitude to you for helping me get to the finish line. I'm filled with great gratitude as I think about Dustin Coleman, Jeffrey Jue, Sean McDowell, Marty Schoenleber, and Dominick Hernández, who read my manuscript drafts. Your love for biblical languages and theology was immensely useful to me and this project. Thanks also to Nick Harrison and Crystal Anderson, who assisted in the flow and smoothing things out. I'm also grateful to all of you who aided in research and finding resources: Joseph Torres, Lour Volkart, Kevin Walker, Connor Ham, Nina Dorsch, Kendall Brewer, and Yoori Hwang (my teaching assistant).

I don't deserve the patience extended to me by my editors at Multnomah as I missed numerous deadlines. Andrew Stoddard, you pursued and got behind this project when all I had was a strong overarching theme and my ideas were like a jigsaw puzzle still in the box. Bruce Nygren, Thomas Womack, Laura Wright, and the rest of the team polished my manuscript and made it come to life.

Rosaria Butterfield, before we connected in 2013, I was beginning to think that I was an anomaly and had to navigate ministry alone. Thank you for blazing the trail between the ditches of orientation change and the idea that same-sex orientation is good. You put up with your "little brother" and my pesky daily texts: "I've got a quick question . . ." Our phone conversations sharpen me, and praying with you enriches my spirit. I'm honored to call you my big sis!

Joe Hendrickson, the Lord in his infinite kindness brought us together as roommates at Moody. You would never have guessed when I picked you up at Midway International Airport in 2002 that I was such a crazy driver and that we would be closest brothers in the Lord sixteen years later. I owe much to you for your courageous honesty and fearless intimacy through all these years.

Alysia Green and Yvonne Foo, my parents and I are exceedingly blessed to have you both as part of our ministry team. Your attention to detail and servant hearts complete our ministry. I love your commitment to the Lord and willingness to go above and beyond. I don't take for granted the effort and time you have both put into our ministry, and I look forward to many more years serving together for the gospel!

Hai-Ray and Lea Meng, Hover Nham, and Joanne Kao, you all have been such great friends to our family and phenomenal supporters. Our best cheerleaders! I'm grateful for your friendship and prayers. You make us feel like one big family!

Steven Yuan, you were always such a good big brother. People ask whether we fought, and no one believes we never did—I've come to realize it had little to do with me. Growing up, we were so different, but you never made me feel like an outsider. I'm delighted to witness God working in you and excited to see what he has in store for you in the years ahead. Don't forget—love Jesus more than life!

Lastly, I'm truly indebted to my parents, Dr. Leon and Angela Yuan. You spoiled me by taking care of many details (cooking, laundry, transportation, etc.) in order that I could focus on writing. Without your persistent exhortations to stay on track, I'd never have finished. Words cannot express how thankful I am that I have such wonderful parents as you. I cannot believe how blessed I am to be able to travel and partner with you both in ministry! You take the loneliness out of being alone. Not only is my conversion directly connected to your faith journey, but my daily sanctification is also directly correlated to your loving me and showing me what "spiritual family" really means.

Dad, you have been my greatest supporter and cheerleader on this project. At times it seemed like your book! Your eyes light up whenever you talk about my book, and it is both embarrassing and heartwarming to hear you passionately boast about me to others. Thanks for loving me and for loving Jesus!

When I was in high school, I had to write a paper on my "hero." All the other students wrote about someone famous: a movie star, a professional sports player, or a historical person. I wrote about my mom and titled it "Mom, My Heroine." Mom, you gave up your full-ride scholarship for a master's degree to do what you really wanted—to be a wife and mother. Then you put Dad through not one but two doctoral programs. While Dad was in school for his second doctorate, you accepted a minimum-wage job as a kidney dialysis tech working the graveyard shift so you could be with me and Steven during the day. You took your role as mother seriously and refused to give it up to someone else.

With your measly salary, you put Dad through school twice and even saved enough for us to buy a house. You built Dad's dental office from the ground up while, at the same time, you combined your keen business sense with your passion for altruism and founded a nonprofit organization that has owned a housing project for low-income seniors for more than thirty years. But all these good works are rubbish compared with the reality that you allowed the Holy Spirit to bring you to the Living Water, accepted the gift of new life, and became a new creation. You strive for perfection and holiness in everything you do. You radiate Christ. You are my heroine, and this book on holiness is dedicated to you.

Notes

Chapter 1: Shaped by God's Grand Story

1. Robert A. J. Gagnon, *The Bible and Homosexual Practice: Texts and Hermeneutics* (Nashville: Abingdon, 2001); Kevin DeYoung, *What Does the Bible Really Teach About Homosexuality?* (Wheaton, IL: Crossway, 2015).

2. Christopher Yuan and Angela Yuan, *Out of a Far Country: A Gay Son's Journey to God, a Broken Mother's Search for Hope* (Colorado Springs: WaterBrook, 2011).

Chapter 2: A Case of Mistaken Identity

1. Matthew Vines, *God and the Gay Christian: The Biblical Case in Support of Same-Sex Relationships* (New York: Convergent Books, 2014), 29, 155.

2. For more on the genesis of sexuality as identity, see Rosaria Champagne Butterfield, *Openness Unhindered: Further Thoughts of an Unlikely Convert on Sexual Identity and Union with Christ* (Pittsburgh: Crown & Covenant, 2015), 94–98.

3. Marc Cortez, *Theological Anthropology: A Guide for the Perplexed* (London: T&T Clark, 2010), 3.

4. David Lomas, *The Truest Thing About You: Identity, Desire, and Why It All Matters* (Colorado Springs: David C Cook, 2014), 69.

5. Michel Foucault, *The History of Sexuality,* trans. Robert Hurley, vol. 1, *An Introduction* (New York: Vintage Books, 1990), 43.

6. Richard von Krafft-Ebing, *Psychopathia Sexualis, with Especial Reference to Contrary Sexual Instinct: A Medico-Legal Study,* trans. Charles Gilbert Chaddock (Philadelphia: F. A. Davis, 1894).

7. Rationalism is the belief that human reason, over against sensory experience, is the only means to attain knowledge and the only judge of truth.

8. John Calvin, *Institutes of the Christian Religion,* ed. John T. McNeill, trans. Ford L. Battles (Louisville: Westminster John Knox, 1960), 37.

Chapter 3: The Image of God

1. For an informative historical survey, see Anthony A. Hoekema, *Created in God's Image* (Grand Rapids: Eerdmans, 1986), 33–65.

2. Moisés Silva, *God, Language, and Scripture: Reading the Bible in the Light of General Linguistics* (Grand Rapids: Zondervan, 1990), 22. Italics in original.

3. Silva, *God, Language, and Scripture,* 22. Italics in original.

4. Bruce K. Waltke, *Genesis: A Commentary* (Grand Rapids: Zondervan, 2001), 65.

5. Wayne Grudem, *Systematic Theology: An Introduction to Biblical Doctrine* (Grand Rapids: Zondervan, 2000), 442.

6. Genesis 1:4, 10, 12, 18, 21, 25.

7. Gerhard von Rad, *Genesis: A Commentary,* rev. ed. (Philadelphia: Westminster, 1961), 52.

8. Kelly M. Kapic, "Anthropology," in *Christian Dogmatics: Reformed Theology for the Church Catholic,* ed. Michael Allen and Scott R. Swain (Grand Rapids: Baker Academic, 2016), 184.

9. Genesis 1:11–12, 21, 24–25. See Genesis 6:20; 7:14.

10. D. J. A. Clines, "The Image of God in Man," *Tyndale Bulletin* 19 (1968), 68–69.

11. Hoekema, *Created in God's Image,* 97; Michael Horton, *The Christian Faith: A Systematic Theology for Pilgrims on the Way* (Grand Rapids: Zondervan, 2011), 380.

12. Richard M. Davidson, *Flame of Yahweh: Sexuality in the Old Testament* (Peabody, MA: Hendrickson, 2007), 18.

13. Mark Sameth, "Is God Transgender?," *New York Times,* August 12, 2016, www.nytimes.com/2016/08/13/opinion/is-god-trans gender.html.

14. Genesis 1:4–5, 7–8, 10–11, 21, 24–25.

15. Hoekema, *Created in God's Image,* 28.

16. Dietrich Bonhoeffer, *The Cost of Discipleship,* trans. R. H. Fuller, ed. Irmgard Booth (New York: Touchstone, 1995), 304.

17. *The Works of John Owen,* ed. William H. Goold, vol. 9, *Sermons to the Church* (Edinburgh: Banner of Truth, 1965), 615.

Chapter 4: The Imprint of Sin

1. John Frame, endorsement in *Adam, the Fall, and Original Sin: Theological, Biblical, and Scientific Perspectives,* ed. Hans Madueme and Michael Reeves (Grand Rapids: Baker Academic, 2014), i.

2. Thomas Boston, *Human Nature in Its Fourfold State* (Edinburgh: Banner of Truth, 1964), 37.

3. Boston, *Human Nature,* 50–51.

4. Victor P. Hamilton, *The Book of Genesis: Chapters 1–17* (Grand Rapids: Eerdmans, 1990), 172.

5. Anthony A. Hoekema, *Created in God's Image* (Grand Rapids: Eerdmans, 1986), 148.

6. R. C. Sproul, *What Is Reformed Theology? Understanding the Basics* (Grand Rapids: Baker Books, 1997), 123.

7. Hoekema, *Created in God's Image,* 143.

8. Augustine, *On Marriage and Concupiscence* 1.27, www.ccel.org /ccel/schaff/npnf105.xvi.v.xxvii.html.

9. Hoekema, *Created in God's Image,* 168.

10. Douglas J. Moo, "'Flesh' in Romans: A Challenge for the Translator," in *The Challenge of Bible Translation: Communicating God's Word to the World,* ed. Glen G. Scorgie, Mark L. Strauss, and Steven M. Voth (Grand Rapids: Zondervan, 2003), 366–67.

11. Thomas R. Schreiner, *Galatians* (Grand Rapids: Zondervan, 2010), 343.

12. John Owen, *Indwelling Sin,* in *Overcoming Sin and Temptation,* ed. Kelly M. Kapic and Justin Taylor (Wheaton, IL: Crossway, 2006), 233–39.

13. John Owen, *Of the Mortification of Sin in Believers,* in *Overcoming Sin and Temptation,* 50.

14. Augustine, *Admonition and Grace,* chap. 33, www.ccel.org/ccel /schaff/npnf105.xx.xxxvi.html.

Chapter 5: Why Anthropology Matters

1. Editors of *Encyclopaedia Britannica*, "Leaning Tower of Pisa," *Encyclopaedia Britannica*, 2017, www.britannica.com/topic /Leaning-Tower-of-Pisa, and *New World Encyclopedia* contributors, "Leaning Tower of Pisa," *New World Encyclopedia*, 2018, www.newworldencyclopedia.org/p/index.php?title=Leaning_Tower _of_Pisa&oldid=1012531.

2. American Psychiatric Association, "LGBT-Sexual Orientation," www.psychiatry.org/lgbt-sexual-orientation (accessed August 10, 2015). As of 2018, without any explanation, this Internet page is no longer available.

Chapter 6: Holy Sexuality

1. Joseph J. Nicolosi, *Shame and Attachment Loss: The Practical Work of Reparative Therapy* (Downers Grove, IL: IVP Academic, 2009), 24.

2. *The New Shorter Oxford English Dictionary on Historical Principles,* ed. Lesley Brown, 4th ed., vol. 2 (New York: Oxford University Press, 1993), s.v. "sexuality."

3. *The Oxford English Dictionary,* 2nd ed. (New York: Oxford University Press, 1989), s.v. "heterosexual."

4. *The Oxford English Dictionary,* 3rd ed. (New York: Oxford University Press, 2000), s.v. "marriage."

Chapter 7: The Temptations

1. William L. Lane, *Hebrews 1–8* (Nashville: Thomas Nelson, 1991), 107; Paul Ellingworth, *The Epistle to the Hebrews: A Commentary on the Greek Text* (Grand Rapids: Eerdmans, 1993), 268; George H. Guthrie, *Hebrews* (Grand Rapids: Zondervan, 1998), 175.

2. Brooke Foss Westcott, *The Epistle to the Hebrews: The Greek Text with Notes and Essays,* 3rd ed. (London: MacMillan, 1920), 59–60.

3. Frederick William Danker, ed., *A Greek-English Lexicon of the New Testament and Other Early Christian Literature,* 3rd ed. (Chicago: University of Chicago Press, 2001), 792–93.

4. John Owen, *Of Temptation: The Nature and Power of It,* in *Overcoming Sin and Temptation,* ed. Kelly M. Kapic and Justin Taylor (Wheaton, IL: Crossway, 2006), 152.

5. David M. Ciocchi, "Understanding Our Ability to Endure Temptation: A Theological Watershed," *Journal of the Evangelical Theological Society* 35, no. 4 (December 1992): 470.

6. Owen, *Of Temptation,* in *Overcoming Sin and Temptation,* 159.

Chapter 8: Anatomy of Desire

1. Augustine, *Confessions* 8.12, www.newadvent.org/fathers/110108 .htm.

2. Augustine, *Confessions* 1.1, www.newadvent.org/fathers/110101.htm.

3. Wesley Hill, "Washed and Still Waiting: An Evangelical Approach to Homosexuality," *Journal of the Evangelical Theological Society* 59, no. 2 (June 2016): 331.

4. Nate Collins, *All but Invisible: Exploring Identity Questions at the Intersection of Faith, Gender, and Sexuality* (Grand Rapids: Zondervan, 2017), 149.

5. Augustine, *Tractates on the First Epistle of John* 4.6, www.new advent.org/fathers/170204.htm.

6. James K. A. Smith, *Desiring the Kingdom: Worship, Worldview, and Cultural Formation* (Grand Rapids: Baker Academic, 2009), 52.

7. Brevard S. Childs, *The Book of Exodus: A Critical, Theological Commentary* (Louisville: Westminster John Knox, 2004), 427.

8. Denny Burk and Heath Lambert, *Transforming Homosexuality: What the Bible Says About Sexual Orientation and Change* (Phillipsburg, NJ: P&R, 2015), 44–45.

9. Simon LeVay, *Gay, Straight, and the Reason Why: The Science of Sexual Orientation,* 2nd ed. (New York: Oxford University Press, 2017), 2.

10. *Merriam-Webster Online Dictionary,* copyright © 2015 by Merriam-Webster Inc., s.v. "platonic."

11. *The Oxford English Dictionary,* 3rd ed. (New York: Oxford University Press, 2010), s.v. "romance."

12. John Piper, *When I Don't Desire God: How to Fight for Joy* (Wheaton, IL: Crossway, 2004), 103.

Chapter 9: "Sexual Orientation"

1. Rosaria Butterfield provides a critical assessment of the concept of sexual orientation. Rosaria Champagne Butterfield, *Openness Unhindered: Further Thoughts of an Unlikely Convert on Sexual*

Identity and Union with Christ (Pittsburgh: Crown & Covenant, 2015), 93–112.

2. James V. Brownson, *Bible, Gender, Sexuality: Reframing the Church's Debate on Same-Sex Relationships* (Grand Rapids: Eerdmans, 2013), 170; Matthew Vines, *God and the Gay Christian: The Biblical Case in Support of Same-Sex Relationships* (New York: Convergent Books, 2014), 106.

3. American Psychological Association, *Answers to Your Questions: For a Better Understanding of Sexual Orientation and Homosexuality* (Washington, DC: APA, 2008), 1.

4. American Psychological Association, *Answers to Your Questions*, 2.

5. *The Yogyakarta Principles: Principles on the Application of International Human Rights Law in Relation to Sexual Orientation and Gender Identity,* March 2007, 6, PDF, http://yogyakarta principles.org/wp-content/uploads/2016/08/principles_en.pdf.

6. Simon LeVay, *Gay, Straight, and the Reason Why: The Science of Sexual Orientation,* 2nd ed. (New York: Oxford University Press, 2017), 1.

7. Douglas J. Moo, *Galatians* (Grand Rapids: Baker Academic, 2013), 344.

8. N. T. Wright, *Paul for Everyone: Romans, Part 1* (Louisville: Westminster John Knox, 2004), 140.

9. Thomas R. Schreiner, *Paul, Apostle of God's Glory in Christ: A Pauline Theology* (Downers Grove, IL: IVP Academic, 2001), 143.

10. Denny Burk and Heath Lambert, *Transforming Homosexuality: What the Bible Says About Sexual Orientation and Change* (Phillipsburg, NJ: P&R, 2015), 50.

11. Moo, *Galatians,* 354.

12. John Piper, *The Pleasures of God: Meditations on God's Delight in Being God,* rev. ed. (Colorado Springs: Multnomah, 2000), 244.

Chapter 10: The Biblical Covenant of Marriage

1. Elisabeth Elliot, *Shadow of the Almighty: The Life and Testament of Jim Elliot* (Peabody, MA: Hendrickson, 2008), 290–91.

2. Timothy Keller, *Counterfeit Gods: The Empty Promises of Money, Sex, and Power, and the Only Hope That Matters* (New York: Penguin, 2016), xix.

3. Christopher Ash, *Marriage: Sex in the Service of God* (Vancouver, BC, Canada: Regent College Publishing, 2003), 127.

4. Obergefell v. Hodges, 576 U.S. 772 F. 3d 388 (2015).

5. Obergefell v. Hodges, 576 U.S. 772 F. 3d 388 (2015).

6. Victor P. Hamilton, *The Book of Genesis: Chapters 1–17* (Grand Rapids: Eerdmans, 1990), 175.

7. Ash, *Marriage*, 115.

8. Jay E. Adams, *Marriage, Divorce, and Remarriage in the Bible: A Fresh Look at What Scripture Teaches* (Grand Rapids: Zondervan, 1980), 8. Italics in original.

9. M. Blaine Smith, *Should I Get Married?*, rev. ed. (Downers Grove, IL: InterVarsity, 2000), 22.

10. Ash, *Marriage*, 119.

11. Matthew Vines, *God and the Gay Christian: The Biblical Case in Support of Same-Sex Relationships* (New York: Convergent Books, 2014), 47.

12. Paul Avis, *Eros and the Sacred* (New York: Morehouse, 1989), 147.

13. Adams, *Marriage, Divorce, and Remarriage*, 8.

14. Ash, *Marriage*, 122.

15. Ludwig Koehler and Walter Baumgartner, *The Hebrew and Aramaic Lexicon of the Old Testament*, revised by Walter Baumgartner and Johann Jakob Stamm (Boston: Brill, 2001), 1:811.

16. Ash, *Marriage*, 120.

17. Allen P. Ross, *Introducing Biblical Hebrew* (Grand Rapids: Baker Academic, 2001), 164.

18. Numbers 3:7–8; 8:26; 18:7; Deuteronomy 11:16; 12:30; 13:4; Joshua 22:5; 1 Kings 9:6; Jeremiah 16:11; Malachi 3:14.

19. G. K. Beale, *The Temple and the Church's Mission: A Biblical Theology of the Dwelling Place of God* (Downers Grove, IL: IVP Academic, 2004), 66–80; G. K. Beale, *A New Testament Biblical Theology: The Unfolding of the Old Testament in the New* (Grand Rapids: Baker Academic, 2011), 617–21.

20. Andrew J. Schmutzer, *Be Fruitful and Multiply: A Crux of Thematic Repetition in Genesis 1–11* (Eugene, OR: Wipf & Stock, 2009), 193.

21. Ash, *Marriage,* 129.

22. James V. Brownson, *Bible, Gender, Sexuality: Reframing the Church's Debate on Same-Sex Relationships* (Grand Rapids: Eerdmans, 2013), 9–13.

23. Brownson, *Bible, Gender, Sexuality,* 29–31; 32–34; repeated in a nonscholarly format in Vines, *God and the Gay Christian,* 144.

24. Brownson, *Bible, Gender, Sexuality,* 30.

25. Genesis 1:4–5, 7–8, 10–11, 16, 21, 25, 27.

26. Schmutzer, *Be Fruitful and Multiply,* 187.

27. Andrew Perriman, *Speaking of Women: Interpreting Paul* (Leicester, UK: Apollos, 1998), 180.

28. Dennis P. Hollinger, *The Meaning of Sex: Christian Ethics and the Moral Life* (Grand Rapids: Baker Academic, 2009), 98.

Chapter 11: A Theology of Marriage

1. The original source for these children's sayings on love is elusive. Elayne Savage, in *Breathing Room: Creating Space to Be a Couple*

(Oakland: New Harbinger, 2000), 12–13, credits the compilation to "Mary Ophanie P. Siatan, in the Philippine *Daily Inquirer.*"

2. Andreas J. Köstenberger with David W. Jones, *God, Marriage, and Family: Rebuilding the Biblical Foundation,* 2nd ed. (Wheaton, IL: Crossway, 2010), 76.

3. Walter Brueggemann, "Of the Same Flesh and Bone (Gn 2,23a)," *Catholic Biblical Quarterly* 32, no. 4 (October 1970): 533–34, 539.

4. Brueggemann, "Of the Same Flesh and Bone," 534–35.

5. Dennis P. Hollinger, *The Meaning of Sex: Christian Ethics and the Moral Life* (Grand Rapids: Baker Academic, 2009), 98.

6. Richard M. Davidson, "The Theology of Sexuality in the Beginning: Genesis 1–2," *Andrews University Seminary Studies* 26, no. 1 (Spring 1988): 22.

7. R. T. France, *The Gospel of Mark: A Commentary on the Greek Text* (Grand Rapids: Eerdmans, 2002), 392. Italics in original.

8. Richard M. Davidson, "Condemnation and Grace: Polygamy and Concubinage in the Old Testament," *Christian Research Journal* 38, no. 5 (2015): 35.

9. For an excellent discussion of every instance of polygamy in the Old Testament, see Davidson, *Flame of Yahweh,* 177–212.

10. John Chrysostom, *Homiliae in Matthaeum* 62.1, www.newadvent.org/fathers/200162.htm.

11. John Nolland, *The Gospel of Matthew: A Commentary on the Greek Text* (Grand Rapids: Eerdmans, 2005), 773.

12. France, *Gospel of Mark,* 387.

13. David P. Gushee, *Changing Our Mind: A Call from America's Leading Evangelical Ethics Scholar for Full Acceptance of LGBT Christians in the Church* (Canton, MI: Read the Spirit Books, 2014), 83–85.

14. Isaiah 54:5; 61:10; 62:5; Jeremiah 3:20; Hosea 2:16.

15. Greg Beale and Ben Gladd have an excellent work on the biblical theology of mystery. Their explanation of Ephesians 5 is highly commendable. I would only slightly differ in that, in Ephesians 5:32, Paul is emphasizing not only continuity but also discontinuity by keeping Israel, the bride of Yahweh, and the church, the bride of Christ, distinct. This is consistent with Ephesians 2:11–21, when Paul says they are "one" but still refers to them as distinctly "both." G. K. Beale and Benjamin L. Gladd, *Hidden but Now Revealed: A Biblical Theology of Mystery* (Downers Grove, IL: IVP Academic, 2014), 173–83.

16. Beale and Gladd, *Hidden but Now Revealed,* 181.

17. John Piper, *This Momentary Marriage: A Parable of Permanence* (Wheaton, IL: Crossway, 2009), 52.

Chapter 12: Singleness

1. Dennis P. Hollinger, *The Meaning of Sex: Christian Ethics and the Moral Life* (Grand Rapids: Baker Academic, 2009), 15.

2. The Westminster Divines, *The Shorter Catechism with Scripture Proofs* (Carlisle: Banner of Truth Trust, 1998), 3. Originally published in 1648.

3. United States Census Bureau, "Marital Status of People 15 Years and Over, by Age, Sex, and Personal Earnings: 2016," www.census .gov/data/tables/2016/demo/families/cps-2016.html.

4. Mark Driscoll, *Religion Saves: And Nine Other Misconceptions* (Wheaton, IL: Crossway, 2009), 186.

5. Harvey McArthur, "Celibacy in Judaism at the Time of Christian Beginnings," *Andrews University Seminary Studies* 25, no. 2 (Summer 1987): 163.

6. J. R. Soza, "Jeremiah," in *New Dictionary of Biblical Theology: Exploring the Unity & Diversity of Scripture,* ed. T. Desmond Alexander et al. (Downers Grove, IL: IVP Academic, 2000), 224.

7. J. A. Thompson, *The Book of Jeremiah* (Grand Rapids: Eerdmans, 1980), 403.

8. Barry Danylak, *Redeeming Singleness: How the Storyline of Scripture Affirms the Single Life* (Wheaton, IL: Crossway, 2010), 71. I owe much to Danylak's extraordinary resources on a biblical theology of singleness.

9. Danylak, *Redeeming Singleness,* 69.

10. Danylak, *Redeeming Singleness,* 108.

11. Danylak, *Redeeming Singleness,* 126; Barry Danylak, *A Biblical Theology of Singleness* (Cambridge: Grove, 2007), 26.

12. Danylak, *Biblical Theology of Singleness,* 26, 166.

13. Danylak, *Biblical Theology of Singleness,* 3.

Chapter 13: More on Singleness

1. Mishnah, Avot 5.21; Babylonian Talmud, Qiddushin 29b.

2. Babylonian Talmud, Yebamot 63b.

3. D. A. Carson, Walter W. Wessel, and Walter L. Liefeld, *Matthew,* in *The Expositor's Bible Commentary* 8, ed. Frank E. Gaebelein (Grand Rapids: Zondervan, 1984), 419.

4. Barry Danylak, *Redeeming Singleness: How the Storyline of Scripture Affirms the Single Life* (Wheaton, IL: Crossway, 2010), 152.

5. Moisés Silva, ed., *The New International Dictionary of New Testament Theology and Exegesis,* 2nd ed. (Grand Rapids: Zondervan, 2014), 2:327.

6. Danylak, *Redeeming Singleness,* 157.

7. John Nolland, *The Gospel of Matthew: A Commentary on the Greek Text* (Grand Rapids: Eerdmans, 2005), 776n40.

8. Carson et al., *Matthew,* 419; R. T. France, *The Gospel of Matthew* (Grand Rapids: Eerdmans, 2007), 723; Craig L. Blomberg, *Matthew* (Nashville: Broadman, 1992), 294.

9. Compare nearly identical phrases in Matthew 11:15 and 13:43.

10. Also see Jeremiah 5:21 and Ezekiel 12:2.

11. Nolland, *Gospel of Matthew,* 531–33.

12. Darrell L. Bock, *Luke,* vol. 2, *9:51–24:53* (Grand Rapids: Baker Academic, 1996), 1623.

13. Robert H. Stein, *Luke* (Nashville: Broadman, 1992), 502.

14. Danylak, *Redeeming Singleness,* 165.

15. Barry Danylak, *A Biblical Theology of Singleness* (Cambridge: Grove, 2007), 27.

16. Danylak, *Redeeming Singleness,* 178.

17. Danylak, *Redeeming Singleness,* 182–85.

18. Barry Danylak, "Secular Singleness and Paul's Response in 1 Corinthians 7," (PhD diss., University of Cambridge, 2011), 152–55.

19. Dale B. Martin, *The Corinthian Body* (New Haven, CT: Yale University Press, 1995), xv.

20. Walter Schmithals, *Gnosticism in Corinth,* trans. John E. Steely (New York: Abingdon, 1971), 221–22, 387–88.

21. Danylak, "Secular Singleness," 3.

22. Gordon D. Fee, *The First Epistle to the Corinthians* (Grand Rapids: Eerdmans, 1987), 309.

23. Fee, *First Epistle,* 309–11; David E. Garland, *1 Corinthians* (Grand Rapids: Baker Academic, 2003), 299.

24. A. W. Richard Sipe, *Celibacy in Crisis: A Secret World Revisited* (New York: Routledge, 2003), 29–39.

25. C. Peter Wagner, *Your Spiritual Gifts Can Help Your Church Grow,* rev. ed. (Ventura: Regal, 2012), 63.

26. Albert Y. Hsu, *Singles at the Crossroads: A Fresh Perspective on Christian Singleness* (Downers Grove, IL: InterVarsity, 1997), 50–51.

27. Garland, *1 Corinthians,* 273.

28. John Owen, *Of the Mortification,* in *Overcoming Sin and Temptation,* ed. Kelly M. Kapic and Justin Taylor (Wheaton, IL: Crossway, 2006), 47.

29. Garland, *1 Corinthians,* 271.

30. Hsu, *Singles at the Crossroads,* 56–58.

31. Hsu, *Singles at the Crossroads,* 58, 60–61.

Chapter 14: Spiritual Family

1. *Stand by Me,* directed by Rob Reiner, Columbia Pictures, 1986.

2. Tom Horner, *Jonathan Loved David: Homosexuality in Biblical Times* (Philadelphia: Westminster, 1978), 26–39; John Boswell, *Same-Sex Unions in Premodern Europe* (New York: Vintage, 1995), 135–37; Daniel A. Helminiak, *What the Bible Really Says About Homosexuality,* rev. ed. (Tajique, NM: Alamo Square, 2000), 123–27; Saul M. Olyan, "'Surpassing the Love of Women': Another Look at 2 Samuel 1:26 and the Relationship of David and Jonathan," in *Authorizing Marriage? Canon, Tradition, and Critique in the Blessing of Same-Sex Unions,* ed. Mark D. Jordan (Princeton: Princeton University Press, 2006), 7–16.

3. Robert A. J. Gagnon, *The Bible and Homosexual Practice: Texts and Hermeneutics* (Nashville: Abingdon, 2001), 146–54.

4. Barry Danylak, *Redeeming Singleness: How the Storyline of Scripture Affirms the Single Life* (Wheaton, IL: Crossway, 2010), 64.

5. John Piper, *This Momentary Marriage: A Parable of Permanence* (Wheaton, IL: Crossway, 2009), 111.

6. Barry Danylak, *A Biblical Theology of Singleness* (Cambridge: Grove, 2007), 27–28.

7. Deuteronomy 32:6; 2 Samuel 7:14; 1 Chronicles 17:13; 22:10; 28:6; Psalm 68:5; 89:26; Isaiah 63:16; 64:8; Jeremiah 3:4, 19; 31:9; Malachi 1:6; 2:10.

8. Robert H. Stein, "Fatherhood of God," in *Evangelical Dictionary of Biblical Theology,* ed. Walter A. Elwell (Grand Rapids: Baker Books, 1996), 247.

9. Joseph H. Hellerman, *When the Church Was a Family: Recapturing Jesus' Vision for Authentic Christian Community* (Nashville: B&H, 2009), 37–38.

10. Rosaria Champagne Butterfield, *The Gospel Comes with a House Key: Practicing Radically Ordinary Hospitality in Our Post-Christian World* (Wheaton, IL: Crossway, 2018), 116–17.

Chapter 15: Sanctification

1. Giorgio Vasari, *The Life of Michelangelo,* trans. A. B. Hinds, rev. ed. (London: Pallas Athene, 2013), 36.

2. Vasari, *Life of Michelangelo,* 197.

3. John N. Oswalt, *The Book of Isaiah: Chapters 1–39* (Grand Rapids: Eerdmans, 1986), 180.

4. John Owen also uses "evangelical holiness." For a good articulation of this, see Kelly M. Kapic, "Evangelical Holiness: Assumptions in John Owen's Theology of Christian Spirituality," in *Life in the Spirit: Spiritual Formation in Theological Perspective,* ed. Jeffrey P. Greenman and George Kalantzis (Downers Grove, IL: IVP Academic, 2010), 97–114.

5. Kapic, "Evangelical Holiness," 101–3.

6. For a helpful chapter on sanctification and its place in soteriology and union with Christ, see Marcus Peter Johnson, "Sanctification in Christ," in *One with Christ: An Evangelical Theology of Salvation* (Wheaton, IL: Crossway, 2013), 115–44.

7. Johnson, *One with Christ,* 116–17.

8. Johnson, *One with Christ,* 125.

Chapter 16: Bad Fruit on Vines

1. Homer, *The Odyssey,* trans. Robert Fitzgerald (New York: Farrar, Straus and Giroux, 1998), 215.

2. Matthew Vines, *God and the Gay Christian: The Biblical Case in Support of Same-Sex Relationships* (New York: Convergent Books, 2014), 12, 19.

3. Vines, *God and the Gay Christian,* 14.

4. David M. Fergusson, L. John Horwood, and Annette L. Beautrais, "Is Sexual Orientation Related to Mental Health Problems and Suicidality in Young People?" *Archives of General Psychiatry* 56, no. 10 (October 1999): 876–80; Richard Herrell et al., "Sexual Orientation and Suicidality: A Co-Twin Control Study in Adult Men," *Archives of General Psychiatry* 56, no. 10 (October 1999): 867–74.

5. Brandon Hatmaker, "Where I stand on LGBTQ . . . ," Facebook, November 1, 2016, www.facebook.com/HatmakerBrandon/posts /661677820673474.

6. Ann P. Haas et al., "Suicide and Suicide Risk in Lesbian, Gay, Bisexual, and Transgender Populations: Review and Recommendations," *Journal of Homosexuality* 58, no. 1 (January 2011): 22.

7. Ron de Graaf, Theo G. M. Sandfort, and Margreet ten Have, "Suicidality and Sexual Orientation: Differences Between Men and Women in a General Population-Based Sample from the

Netherlands," *Archives of Sexual Behavior* 35, no. 3 (June 2006): 253.

8. European Commission, *Special Eurobarometer 437: Discrimination in the EU in 2015* (Brussels: European Union, 2015), 50.

9. John Nolland, *The Gospel of Matthew: A Commentary on the Greek Text* (Grand Rapids: Eerdmans, 2005), 336–37.

Chapter 17: Compassion

1. Darrell L. Bock, *Luke,* vol. 2, *9:51–24:53* (Grand Rapids: Baker Academic, 1996), 1031.

2. Bock, *Luke,* 1021.

3. Christopher Yuan, *Giving a Voice to the Voiceless: A Qualitative Study of Reducing Marginalization of Lesbian, Gay, Bisexual, and Same-Sex Attracted Students at Christian Colleges and Universities* (Eugene, OR: Wipf & Stock, 2016).

Chapter 18: Outreach

1. Oswald Chambers, *My Utmost for His Highest: Selections for the Year* (New York: Dodd, Mead, 1935), 219.

2. Chris Fabry, *War Room: Prayer Is a Powerful Weapon* (Carol Stream, IL: Tyndale, 2015), 172.

Chapter 19: Receiving the News

1. "The State of the Church 2016," Barna Group, September 15, 2016, www.barna.com/research/state-church-2016.

2. This is a very helpful and concise book on homosexuality. It's a quick read, summarizing both biblical and practical matters. Sam Allberry, *Is God Anti-Gay? And Other Questions About Homosexuality, the Bible and Same-Sex Attraction,* rev. ed. (Epsom, UK: Good Book, 2015).

Chapter 20: Discipleship

1. Erwin W. Lutzer, *Putting Your Past Behind You: Finding Hope for Life's Deepest Hurts,* rev. ed. (Chicago: Moody, 1997), 49.

2. Mark Dever, *Discipling: How to Help Others Follow Jesus* (Wheaton, IL: Crossway, 2016), 68–69.

3. Tony Evans, *Tony Evans' Book of Illustrations: Stories, Quotes, and Anecdotes from More Than 30 Years of Preaching and Public Speaking* (Chicago: Moody, 2009), 88–89.

About the Author

Dr. Christopher Yuan has taught the Bible at Moody Bible Institute for over ten years, and his speaking ministry on faith and sexuality has reached five continents. He speaks at conferences, on college campuses, and in churches. He has coauthored with his mother their memoir (now in seven languages), *Out of a Far Country: A Gay Son's Journey to God, a Broken Mother's Search for Hope*, and he is also the author of *Giving a Voice to the Voiceless*. Christopher graduated from Moody Bible Institute in 2005, Wheaton College Graduate School in 2007 with a master of arts in biblical exegesis, and Bethel Seminary in 2014 with a doctor of ministry degree.

Praise for *Out of a Far Country*...

"*Christopher Yuan and Angela Yuan have told the story of their miraculous journey from broken lives, relationships, and dreams to a place of hope and healing.* Out of a Far Country *brings home the living truth that in the midst of a broken and hurting world, God is at work to redeem, renew, and reconcile his beloved. I'm particularly happy to endorse this book because Christopher, like myself, was broken in prison and redeemed by Christ.*"

—CHUCK COLSON, founder of Prison Fellowship and the Chuck Colson Center for Christian Worldview

"*The story of Angela Yuan and Christopher Yuan,* Out of a Far Country, *will minister rich grace and hope to mothers who are praying for the return of a prodigal, to the prodigals they love, and to anyone battling a sinful addiction that seems impossible to overcome. This is a deeply moving account of God's amazing power and love.*"

—NANCY LEIGH DEMOSS, best-selling author, host of the Revive Our Hearts radio program

"*The Good Shepherd knows his sheep and calls them by name. Christopher Yuan, trapped in a life of drugs and sexual addiction, heard that call and rose to follow Jesus. His and his mother's account of that rising is a profound story of redemption that all of us in this broken generation need to hear.*"

—DUANE LITFIN, president emeritus of Wheaton College in Illinois

Christopher Yuan is a passionate speaker, delivering life-changing messages to audiences young and old. Gripping the audience with raw honesty and transparency, Christopher's journey from tragedy to triumph has moved and warmed countless hearts. His dynamic messages inspire people from all walks of life, all around the world.

Request to have Christopher come speak to your church, ministry, or organization! More info at ChristopherYuan.com

CONNECT WITH CHRISTOPHER YUAN

Visit ChristopherYuan.com or follow Christopher on Facebook, Twitter, and YouTube!

 @christopheryuan

 @christopheryuan

 @christopheryuan